HOW TO SUCCEED IN THE BUSINESS OF FINDING A JOB

HOW TO SUCCEED IN THE BUSINESS OF FINDING A JOB

Phoebe Taylor

nh Nelson-Hall Publishers Chicago

Library of Congress Cataloging in Publication Data

Taylor, Phoebe.
    How to succeed in the business of finding a job.

        1. Applications for positions. 2. Vocational
guidance. I. Title
HF5383.T3   650'.14   74-17812
ISBN 0-88229-162-9

Manufactured in the United States of America

CONTENTS

PREFACE

How To Succeed in the Business of Finding a Job is a psychologically oriented approach to hiring and being hired. It takes a broad view of employment, from the job seeker's need for self-understanding to an inside look at employers' hiring practices.

For more than fifteen years as an employment counselor, I have been matching the needs of job seekers with the needs of employers. My experience has made me keenly aware of the necessity for both the candidates and the people who hire other people to evaluate themselves before they evaluate each other.

This book gives insights to individuals on both sides of the hiring desk by analyzing and interpreting their methods and motives. It takes job seekers behind the scenes on a journey that will give them a perspective on employers' hiring problems and techniques—a perspective that will help them launch a more informed and more successful job search campaign.

Every job seeker must begin his or her search with a searching look within. Nobody but you can identify your real preferences and needs. That means asking yourself basic questions concerning your interests and priorities. After all, a job search is just as much a search for one's self-image as it is for employment.

Whether you want a job, a better position, or a satisfying career, this book is written to help you achieve your goal. To that end, it introduces two new job guidance tools: the Selectascope and the Perceptual Résumé.

The Selectascope will help you determine the marketable job qualifications you have to offer, who needs them, and how to make them wanted.

The Perceptual Résumé is a résumé format that stresses the similarities between the skills you offer and the positions you seek.

It is my hope that you will find in these pages the understanding, support, and confidence that everyone needs to accomplish his or her goal. If this book helps you realize the fullness of your potential, then my purpose in writing it will have been served.

I am most in debt to Harry David for the valuable advice and assistance he gave to bring this book to its present form. I owe much gratitude to Anita Dougherty, Dr. William Stuart, Jeanne Hale, and Pierre Dowd for their professional counsel. My thanks go to Katherine Fisher, who has been a source of encouragement, and to Jean Choate for the tender, loving care she gave the preparation of this manuscript. Beyond that, I am deeply grateful to my husband and family, who shared with me this venture into print.

PART 1: PSYCHOLOGICAL ASPECTS OF THE JOB SEARCH

Which came first: you or your career?

For more than fifteen years I have helped people find solutions to job problems.

"How did I ever get stuck in retailing?" an assistant buyer asks.

"There's no future in college teaching," an instructor announces.

"I want a professional job with travel," a secretary insists.

"If I had it to do over again, I'd be a veterinarian," confesses a statistician.

How fortunate that we found each other. Given your talent to do a job and mine to find one, we are fitting partners in this business called employment. Let me introduce you to my philosophy of searching for a job and to the dynamics of the marketplace.

The route to the job of your choice begins with a searching inward look. Only *then* seek a work situation compatible with your personality and pattern of behavior. This book is a study of the relationship between who you are and what you do and between those who hire and those who are hired.

Occupation is more than employment. It's not just a nine to five activity for which you get paid. Whether you consider your occupation to be a job, a position, or a career, it should reflect your basic interests, attitudes, and values. You owe it to yourself to be in a work situation that satisfies these requirements. Work is an integral part of your life. It mirrors your self-image and hopefully provides one outlet for self-expression. Job functions must suit your innate characteristics and personality traits. These factors are often far more important than what you studied in college or how many years of experience you have.

These subtle, intangible qualities are really the stuff that matters in your work—whatever kind it is. Behavior patterns are your compass to finding a job, and you should set your sights on the job that allows you to be yourself—whatever the field, whatever your role. Add this dimension to your job requirements and this insight to your search, and you will take a giant step toward job satisfaction.

Most people start looking for a job or considering a job change by gazing through the wrong end of the telescope. People define employment in terms of job titles and occupational categories when it should be defined in terms of behavior and personality traits. For example, certain writing skills are standard requirements

2

for some jobs in advertising. Writers who choose advertising careers, however, must also work well under pressure, write persuasively, and relate to the business world. Others with writing skill may be technical writers, newscasters, poets, or any one of forty other kinds of professional writers. But the copywriter is in advertising primarily because that field serves best his inner needs, not just his pocketbook.

Another typical job hunting problem—almost an occupational hazard in itself—is the language used to describe work. People continually mouth clichés to express job goals, thereby creating rather than explaining the problem. Using generalities instead of specifics does not advance your cause. Have you ever heard yourself say to a prospective employer, "I want an interesting job with responsibility and challenge"? Did you ever honestly ask yourself, "What *really* interests me? Responsibility for *what*, specifically?" And, by the way, "Just who challenges whom?"

Every occupation offers an opportunity for you to express your personality, and you can expect your share of challenge, interest, and responsibility from every job. And to every job you hope to bring your abilities—creative, administrative, managerial. Since similar job functions exist in different fields, don't be distracted by the hocus-pocus of job titles or descriptive adjectives. The actual content and context of the job are what count.

Your concern should be whether you are going to do what best suits your own individual characteristics—as a technician in a hospital, an accountant in a department store, or a social worker in a day care center. For example, some technicians are excellent organizers, while others are creative thinkers; some accountants are best at problem-solving, others at communicating with clients; some social workers bring objectivity to the job, while some contribute sensitivity. Every profession has room for a variety of talents.

Your personality traits and behavior patterns existed long before you ever thought of working. They influenced your initial career choice and are now the guides to work situations in which you perform best. For instance, those who are organized and disciplined can thrive in a structured atmosphere that would stifle some people who are impulsive and original. These inner characteristics are important determinants of job satisfaction and the primary motivation for job change. Don't even begin to look for a job until you're sure you know your own traits.

The hardest part of any job is finding it

Neither time nor place can still these refrains:

"Tell me, where are all the jobs?" asks a recent University of Pennsylvania grad plaintively.

"I've been job hunting for four months. I can't believe with all my experience there isn't a good one out there for me," complains a public relations executive.

"This is devastating," says an administrative assistant. "Is it me—or the economy?"

An editor reports that never before did she have a problem getting a job. Yet she sent off a dozen résumés in different directions and failed to uncover a single possibility.

When I hear comments like these over and over again from competent men and women, it makes me realize that no one ever becomes an expert at finding a job. It isn't something you make a career of—but a career from. For many, the job of getting a job is demanding, discouraging, demeaning, depressing, and disappointing. It is fraught with frustration. The fortunate few who've never experienced this trauma should return this book unread or pass it along to a friend in need.

Job-hunting can be a traumatic experience for any number of reasons, and until you isolate the specific factors particular to your personal needs, your search will be fruitless. The university grad went to work as soon as he identified his real job objectives. The PR expert found employment after he learned how to market himself in interviews for a PR position. Major surgery had to be performed on the administrative assistant's résumé, and, then she, too, landed a job. When the editor put aside certain preconceptions and applied for the managing editor's slot on a competitor's staff, she was hired. Just minor corrections had major consequences for each one's career.

Launching your campaign demands careful planning and strategy whether you are seeking a job or a job change. If you're unemployed, you will be suffering more stress in already stressful circumstances. How ironic that just when you need to be at your best, you're not.

Here are a few suggestions to help you cope with your plight. Don't go into isolation. Stay in touch with friends and colleagues, both for their support and for their suggestions. Above all, remember that somebody out there wants you—and needs you! Keep your

4

perspective. Total preoccupation with finding the right occupation may be dangerous to your mental health. Work at your hobby. Don't lose your sense of humor.

That's easier said than done, of course, for a job is intricately woven into the very fabric of your life. To have income stop while mortgage and car payments go on, to feel anxious when you must project confidence, to suffer the slings and arrows of social pressures while nursing a wounded ego, to be physically spent just when your physiological system should be working to capacity—all this complicates an already distressing situation. How you go about finding employment reveals something about yourself—your drive, stamina, seriousness, patience, and resourcefulness.

The need for instant employment is a special problem. Its solution lies in setting short-range goals to meet immediate needs and letting time be your ally in achieving long-range objectives. The very existence of a long-range plan makes the acceptance of expedient employment bearable, gives you something to strive for, and increases hope for a better future.

Yet there is a difference between just any job and the right job. You may have the former now or find it with little difficulty. Fulfilling career objectives, however, requires mastering the game plan spelled out in the following pages.

Identify your job preferences and needs

Design a job search aimed at achieving your most important priority.

Compare job hunting with shopping. When you purchase a coat, you choose one that is the proper size and is made of a suitable fabric, has a flattering style, and has the right price tag attached. It's you! So it is with finding a job, except the words are different. Does your experience fit? Is the salary acceptable? Does the job reflect the image you have of yourself? Is it *you?*

Put into vocational jargon, we're talking about *job criteria*—factors to evaluate when considering a position. These are the common denominators that exist for anyone, any time a job change is made:

Professional growth
Responsibility
Advancement opportunity
Security

Salary
Benefits
Recognition
Prestige
Location

Each criterion means something different to each person, and the importance you give to each one is the first clue to identifying your career priorities.

Sheila Myer had been on the editorial staff of a university press for five years, and when a man from outside was hired to fill the assistant editorship she had been eyeing, she resigned. Crushed at being passed over, she was determined to seek elsewhere the recognition she had been denied.

Sheila suddenly found herself on the job market, and it was like being lost in a strange city without a street map. Don't push the panic button, she told herself. Be calm. Act—don't react!

First she quickly updated her old résumé—too quickly, unfortunately. She did not realize that it takes a lot of soul-searching and deliberation to prepare a résumé that will open the right doors for you. She sent out résumés to vie for positions as a television scriptwriter, managing editor of a magazine, PR assistant in a consumer product corporation. There were jobs out there, and she knew she was good. Why should she have trouble landing one?

If Sheila's top priority for her next job was to enjoy the recognition she felt she deserved, then it was necessary that she bring her credentials to the attention of *employers who needed and respected her expertise.* Not to PR departments, which have an entirely different approach to communications from Sheila's. Not to the TV media, which require a specific type of talent. Nor even to magazines, whose pace differs vastly from that of book editing.

Finally, Sheila took stock and realized that the folks who were going to respect her professionalism most were those who did what she did. She called the executive editor of a college textbook house. When they met, it was like a get-together of a mutual admiration society. They clicked. Now it's hard to tell who's happier—the executive editor or his new managing editor, Sheila Myer.

What do you really want to do?

Plan first—act later. The search for a job should begin with an inward look. How can you find anything unless you know what you're looking for? And how do you know *that* until you become acquainted with yourself?

Before you generate a frenzy of job-hunting activity that merely creates heat without shedding light, take some time to get to know yourself. Allow some intrinsic questions to surface, difficult as it may be. The truth is always a little frightening (but so enlightening). Ask yourself:

> What do I expect a job to do for me? (and vice versa)
> What gives me the most satisfaction?
> What are my assets?
> What are my liabilities?
> What are my achievements?
> What were the plusses and minuses of my previous jobs?
> What is my motivation—money, job interest, status?
> What is my self-image?
> What organizations do I identify with?

One person I counseled, Kenneth Bunting, told me about such a soul-searching session, and from the way he described it, it went something like this:

"I've got to get out of Marcy's department store," he told himself. "I'm going buggy. I can't stand retailing anymore!"

He had been there for two years. What had turned him off?

"I've had it. No more six-day week. I want a normal, five-day week like everybody else. Is that unreasonable? And there's nowhere for me to go unless the buyer dies or leaves. She's not leaving, and she doesn't look as if she's dying, either."

Still, what had kept him there for two years?

"Darned if I know. I tried to find some job related to European history, my college major. The subject interests me, but I haven't been able to put it to practical use in terms of a career."

He could teach, he told himself.

"But I have no ed courses. Anyhow, whom am I kidding? I don't really want to teach."

What did he really want to do? Something had kept him in sheets, blankets, and bedding for two years.

"I used to think I could help the customer get the best deal for his money and that we could make a profit besides. But it's just a rat race."

Had he done anything satisfying at all?

"Last year I did an inventory report for the internal security department. Worked on percentages of merchandise lost, stolen, and returned. What an eye-opener!"

What was it about doing the report that he had liked?

"Well, the figures told a story; something should have come out of that report. The amount of shoplifting and pilfering going on is unbelievable. I've got ideas to plug those losses that would make security sit up and listen."

So maybe he should see about changing positions in his company.

"But I want to get out of retailing and try something new. I expected to set policy someday. But I'm no closer to that goal. I'm at a dead end."

But the retailing field has other kinds of jobs that might interest him. Why take a radical step when there may be a reasonable solution? Why not start with changing his job before switching to another field?

"I suppose before I think about handing in my resignation I should see the people upstairs. I'll try to convince them that I have the ability to solve problems that involve inventory and distribution. I guess the first step is sorting out my thoughts."

Not everyone will find such ready and immediate solutions to his job problems, but you can make no progress until you subject yourself to some keen self-analysis and self-evaluation.

Find yourself before you find a job

It was a deep voice, a little anxious, talking to me on the telephone, telling me more than I wanted to know.

". . . Henry Waltower, degree from the University of Pennsylvania, political science major, graduated 1969. What kind of jobs do you have?"

I wondered which of the hundreds I knew about might be appropriate.

He said he had worked as an advance man for McCarthy —Eugene, that is—during the 1968 campaign. He was hired as a technical abstractor by a publisher of textbooks after college, and he thought he'd like PR.

I was afraid to ask why. Instead I asked, "What are you doing now?"

"I'm a cabbie."

8

"What do you want to do?"

"I don't know for sure."

"How can I give career advice over the phone to someone I've never met?"

"Look, do you have any jobs? I've gotten the runaround for three months," he said. No wonder, I thought. He can't make points with that attitude.

"Where have you been looking?"

"Everywhere. I must have tried a hundred places."

"Sounds like you've made a hundred mistakes."

And I heard the phone click.

I was annoyed with myself for being so sarcastic. After all, my job is to help people, not to discourage them. Well, I'm human.

So I was really glad when ten minutes later Henry Waltower was on the line again, and I told him I'd like to help. He came to see me at my office the next day. He had a large chip on his shoulder that implied, "What are *you* going to do for *me*?" But he was eager to tell his story, and I was eager to listen.

"I've been trying to break into public relations," Henry said. "I'll begin anywhere. Sweep the floors, empty wastebaskets, just as long as I get a start. A chance to prove myself. I want a piece of the action."

I needed to know something more specific, so I tried to prod him with this question: "If you're so good at PR, how come you haven't done a better job promoting your own job search?"

"Oh, come on; I've tried everything!"

"That's part of the problem right there, Henry. A search that is more selective is bound to be more productive. It pays to do your homework. It saves time, energy, and money. Why, someone might even be paying you by now."

"I'm making bread driving a hack. But that's all."

"At least no one's breathing down your neck telling you what to do," I said, trying to look on the bright side.

"It gives me a chance to think."

"What do you think about?"

"Oh, how crummy things are. We put men on the moon, but can't put men to work. Pollution may lick us before we lick it. And I wonder if we'll survive what's-his-name's administration."

As he contemplated his concerns about the future, I wanted to know more about his past. A person's background provides a frame of reference for and insights into understanding his characteristics.

"What does your father do?" I asked.

"What difference does that make?"

"Just curious. Every bit of information helps."

"He's a surgeon."

"Brothers? Sisters?"

"My older brother is finishing med school. My sister is married. I'm the youngest."

"And your mother?"

"She works at our community library a few days a week. Volunteers."

"Sometimes the answers to questions like these explain the rationale for a career choice, but I'm still in the dark. Henry, why do you want a job in public relations?"

He said that he thought the only way to change things was through the legislative process, and he wanted to be involved in providing the information needed to make that change.

I asked him what things in particular he wanted to change and what causes he related to.

"It doesn't matter. I could relate to lots of issues—housing, education, consumerism, environment."

"And what would your contribution be?" I asked cautiously.

"Well." He thought further. "Well, what do you mean exactly—contribution?"

"I mean what can you offer such a cause—what skills, talent, know-how do you have?"

"I told you over the phone I organized students for the McCarthy campaign."

"Tell me in detail what you did."

"Well, I organized meetings, arranged for speakers, wrote press releases."

"Was it a satisfying experience?" I asked.

Yes, he had liked it, but he wished he had had more to say about policy and program. "After all, I have a political science degree."

That made me think that his interests might be more issue-oriented than action-oriented. We talked about why he got a degree in political science and whether he had expected to parlay it into a career. I asked about his extracurricular activities. They included debating, student government representative, and assisting in the library.

And so I was beginning to scratch the surface of the real Henry Waltower.

For the record, I described several PR positions I was currently recruiting for. One required strong writing ability, preferably a degree in journalism. Another required multimedia experience. The candidate should have a promotional approach to PR —trade shows, exhibits, conventions.

With each example I ticked off, Henry showed increasing disappointment. "Okay, you've made your point. Forget PR. What then?"

I asked him, "If you could do whatever you wanted — what would it be?"

He thought for a long while and then told me about a term paper he had written for an honors course in labor relations. He thought he was at his best gathering and analyzing data. A job combining those interests would really be meaningful, he told me.

I suggested that he might consider doing research for a labor union and perhaps ultimately becoming an information specialist. Almost immediately he relaxed. A smile lit up his face, which seemed to say, "Why didn't I think of that?"

Now that we both knew what we were looking for, I could begin to help Henry find a job.

I asked to see his résumé. It was three pages, single-spaced. Since he didn't have much experience, why did he need three pages to describe it?

I explained to Henry that the résumé has a limited function—to obtain an invitation for an interview, nothing more, nothing less.

With a blue pencil in my hand, and the reader (a personnel manager) in mind, I quickly crossed out nonessentials (height, weight) from the top of the page. Hobbies and interests were placed where they belong (if they appear at all)—near the end of the résumé.

"Professional skills: managerial ability, good public speaker, ability with all forms of writing." Overdone, I felt, and somewhat inaccurate in any case.

"Professional objective: a responsible permanent position in public relations where my experience and creativity may be fully utilized." Also pretentious and inaccurate. Out! The category on educational background began with high school. Why give priority to insignificant information? Degreed job seekers can allow a high school education to be assumed.

Oops, a typo — that's inexcusable. The résumé is your calling card, an advertising message. A researcher should find facts—and mistakes.

The job seeker must realize that a skilled résumé reader takes less than two minutes to let his eyes search for pertinent data. What personnel is looking for are *facts*. If résumés are to survive keen competition, they must meet the FIRST LAW OF HIRING: Establish the relationship between the applicant's previous experience and the job to be filled.

Henry is going to market himself as a researcher, so his résumé tells about his honors paper on labor relations, his experience of and interest in being a digger for information, a gatherer of data. Pertinent extracurricular activities are added as supportive evidence: library assistant, student government, debating society. The object is to prepare a document as individual as one's fingerprints.

The description of Henry's past position as technical writer for a publishing firm was severely edited. Salary and reason for leaving were eliminated. (Only when this information promotes your cause should it be included.) Constructive comments documenting skills and indicating previous responsibilities were emphasized.

Henry left my office with instructions to return with a brief, specific, positive résumé, concisely written, well organized, and readable. In addition, I asked him to draft a cover letter that would reveal something about his personality, his career direction, and his ability to communicate on paper—a topic to which I shall return later. Also, I asked Henry to prepare a list of prospective employers whose activities coincided with his particular job interests, showing him the directories commonly used, plus Chamber of Commerce literature and trade journals. I suggested that he might get ideas from newspaper business pages or even the front page and told him to scan the Yellow Pages, talk to friends and colleagues, contact his college placement office, try another employment counselor, look in the classified ads.

He left ready for some positive action. When he returned, he had a résumé that reflected both his capabilities and his interests couched in terms aimed at demonstrating his usefulness to an employer. This improvement alone is an ego-boost for any job seeker; it was for Henry. Justifiably, Henry had more confidence now. Having identified his own goals and needs, it became easier to identify organizations compatible with them.

"Well, let me tell you what I've accomplished since our last brain-storming session," he said with an air of authority. "My friend's father is a labor union executive, and I have an appointment to see him next week. I tried my college placement office but didn't turn up anything. I decided not to go to another employment agency; I didn't realize how much help you'd be. Looked in trade journals, but the advertisements specify more experience than I can offer."

He showed me a list of places he now planned to contact: three research firms (only one was involved in social science research, so I eliminated the other two); four unions, two government agencies (scratched because the hiring process is so slow), a congressman on the Labor Relations Committee (dropped at first because Henry wasn't a constituent but added later, just in case), and consulting firms.

I reviewed the cover letter Henry had drafted. It was very good. It fleshed out the facts in the résumé and said that he would make a follow-up phone call to arrange for a personal interview.

Henry had been quick to learn. He even allowed himself to be optimistic, but he realized that the hardest part of a job must be finding it.

"Hiring is always going on," I told him encouragingly.

He surprised me. "Look, here's an ad I clipped out of the classified section; someone is looking for a researcher. It's as if it were written with me in mind. What do you think?"

I studied the one-inch ad:

Research Asst.: Major association seeks an individual with experience in design, implementation, and validation of manpower tests and measurements. Psychology bkgd. helpful. Salary commensurate with exp. Liberal fringe benefits. Box W183.

"Really? This is you? Why?" I asked.

"Come on! It's obvious!" he replied.

"Not to me. What do you think they're looking for?"

"It's only an assistant's position, so you don't need a heck of a lot of experience. Right? It's a manpower study. Well, that falls within the scope of labor relations," he persisted. "And besides, I took three psych courses!"

I reread the little ad once more. It's a shame that in a résumé we have nothing but words to express our thoughts. Everyone gives them a different meaning. This ad was as guilty of vagueness as most résumés are. In fact, it was a perfect example of the games people play. Employers who place such ambiguous ads in the newspapers deserve all the worthless or unrelated résumés they receive. They're responsible for confusing the hiring process and creating a problem where none needs to exist.

In this ad, the *level of responsibility* necessary to qualify for the position is not indicated. Therefore, the job seeker cannot properly evaluate his experience in terms of the employer's need. The duties are not described in detail, so *any* would-be researcher might respond. Salary is not mentioned, compounding the mystery.

What *is* the ad telling us? Somewhere there's a personnel manager, probably short-staffed, using a box number so that he won't have to reply to the hundred-plus résumés he will receive. He wants to test the market and see what's out there, so he writes an ad that's vague and limited in detail. The key words are "design" and "validation," terms easily recognizable by psychometrists or industrial psychologists. Basically that's the background he wants. However, with that ad, he'll receive résumés from some with Psych.101 to their credit and some with Ph.D.'s.

This personnel manager's approach is no different from a job seeker's random try-anything effort. This ad is only a "call for help" without any guarantee that the right person will answer.

You're sending out an SOS also, but it's your responsibility to see to it that the right person in the right organization gets your résumé. Answer that particular ad, and your résumé will be buried under three pounds of competing resumes. You won't be any closer to a job, and you'll have the distinct disadvantage of thinking you've done something constructive.

Would *you* hire *you* for a position requiring, at the very least, familiarity with tests and measurements? Forget it. Now that you've got yourself a good résumé, see that it's eyeballed by someone who needs what you have to offer. That reader will be pleased with what he sees—you've said just the right things. Saying more might lessen his interest. Recruiters look for key phrases to decide whether your background is a possibility for their opening. "Action" words can describe your capabilities: "abstracted," "tabulated," "reported."

"Henry, go home. Have the résumé reproduced on good quality bond stock. Be sure to proof it once more. Send a copy to the organizations on your list; then call me."

Henry called on a Tuesday. "What's next? I sent all the stuff out Friday," he reported.

"Good. Call each contact tomorrow for the sole purpose of setting up an interview—nothing more. Try to avoid being interviewed over the phone. After all you've done, this is no time to be eliminated. You want to get in to see him and you want to be seen by him. Keep in touch."

A happy face was in my office later in the week—Henry had lined up two interviews.

"Who are you going to see?"

"The congressman's administrative assistant Monday morning and the Urban Development Institute in the afternoon."

"That may or may not mean the congressman has a job, but consider the interview a rehearsal for the one at UDI," I commented. "Remember, people hire people whose experience relates to the nature of the work to be done. How you relate to the job and how well you communicate can be decisive. Be yourself. Above all, *listen*. Keep in mind that UDI has a position it wants to fill."

"I think I'll go to the library to get some more information about UDI," Henry told me.

"That's the spirit! And Henry, don't forget—a good man is hard to find. Good luck!"

Several days later I answered my telephone. There was this deep voice, very excited, telling more than I could assimilate in one moment. And the voice was saying, ". . . and I start on the 15th in UDI's Department of Occupational Safety, as a data analyst. Everyone was just great to me. Guess what—the personnel man's a U. of P. grad. Did you hear me? This is Henry."

Who do you think you are?

In your search for self-understanding, it is not sufficient merely to identify job preferences and needs. That's like getting a gift and not opening the package. You've got to look inside. Find out *why* they are your preferences and you'll get more insight into the role you see yourself playing in the working world.

Next you've got to analyze *why* you want to be *what* you want to be. Is it for status, security, salary? Or values, beliefs, commitments? Maybe your career interests were awakened in college or influenced by your father. Perhaps you love to work with other people, or perhaps you crave privacy. Do you love the outdoors, hate detail, have to be home by five? These are some of the things you should know about yourself in order to better understand the basis for your job objective.

Now for an exercise in philosophical gymnastics. In order to separate who you think you are from who you really are, compare your explanation of why you act with what you actually do. To show you how this relates to getting a job, just let me give you a typical example of what I mean.

For the past three years, on the average of once every three months, I've been getting phone calls like this from Peter Sandahl:

"What have you done for me lately? You know you gotta get me out of here."

Regardless of what I tell him about possible job opportunities, Peter's reaction is always negative. "It's too far to travel." (Peter, an engineer for the State Highway and Roads Bureau, leaves his house at 8:17 and is at his desk at 8:31.) "What, no retirement plan?" Some government employees remain on the job because they think a good retirement program is a substitute for a fulfilling job.

Every now and then I give *him* a call. I tell him about a position that requires his expertise in testing materials, or about an opening for a purchasing department chief—the very jobs Peter claims interest him—and he rejects both.

Peter constantly protests that he hates his job. Maybe so, but his actions tell me he really doesn't plan to do a thing about it. Three years from now he'll still be telling me, "You gotta get me out of here. . . ."

There are lots of Peter Sandahls in the world. They like the comfortable nine-to-five routine of their noncommuting jobs. But they also feel guilty. They know they lack ambition.

Are *you* serious enough about *your* career to ask yourself difficult questions and cope with honest answers? It isn't easy, but the answers are necessary.

You've got to know yourself well enough to have the inner confidence to convince a prospective employer that you *can* do what you *want* to do. (After all, he won't know about your abilities until you tell him.) And are you really prepared to "sacrifice" some comforts—as Peter is not—to further your career? The sophisticated employer will not be fooled. Giving an account of yourself in an interview is not just a matter of words; it is also a question of attitude.

I've devoted an entire section to interviews, so for now, let me just introduce you to the cast of characters taking part in the interview scenario. There you are on stage, an aspirant hoping to be chosen for the part. Meanwhile the employer is listening to your lines and waiting for his cue to have his say. By my count, there are six of you—first, who you think you are, who he thinks you are, and who you really are. That leaves who he thinks he is, who you think he is, and who he really is. It's a formidable confrontation!

Job seekers and job givers need to know themselves before they are best able to communicate with each other. Employers need to think before they act, just as employees-to-be must. Personnel is not all-knowing. When corporations hire staff they, too, must analyze their needs and priorities before they put up a Help Wanted sign.

If personnel people recruit without developing guidelines for the job they are trying to fill and the kind of person best suited to fill it, then they have failed in their job. I have assisted employers who really couldn't define the job to be done or describe the person to do it. For example, I have been told initially that the job is director of public affairs; salary: twenty thousand dollars. Two weeks later I'm told the job is assistant director of public affairs; salary: eighteen thousand dollars. The following month they hire an assistant to the director of communications; salary: fifteen thousand. Even worse, after making an exhaustive search for a particular candidate, the decision is made not to fill the position at all! No doubt there are valid reasons for these changes, but it seems to be the better part of wisdom for management to define their needs before they take action.

Similarly, I believe that the more you learn about yourself, the more you'll learn about the job you want. The more you look within, the more you'll know what to look for in a career.

Will you or won't you change?

Everyone wants a fulfilling job and a satisfying career. To achieve this, some people wish to make drastic changes.

I remember one instance in particular. It began with a telephone call.

"I'm looking for an opinion," a voice on the phone was saying.

"That's a new wrinkle," I admitted. "The usual refrain is, 'I'm looking for a job.'"

She laughed. A friend had had kind words for me, she said, and she hoped I could give her some advice, "perhaps over lunch." I accepted her compliment and her invitation, and we met at one of those "in" places downtown.

"Mrs. Taylor, I'm Carole Armstrong," she said, her hand taking a firm grip on mine.

After the usual amenities, she quickly gave me some sketchy details about herself. She'd been treasurer of the Guaranty Trust Bank for seventeen years. Her work was satisfying, she said, but not completely fulfilling. "The banking industry has been good to women," she commented. "They had women officers long before it became the thing to do. I couldn't ask for a better setup than the one I have. It's great as far as it goes, but does it go far enough? That's the question I keep asking myself."

"Do you mean at Guaranty Trust, or in the banking field, or—"

"No," she interrupted. "You see, behind this conservative professional façade, there's another me."

So halfway through sautéed scallops we got to the crux of our meeting.

"I've got a case of Walter-Mitty-itis," Carole confessed. "There's one thing I always thought I'd like to be—a dress designer. Do I sound ridiculous?"

"All kinds of people have all sorts of notions," I assured her. "What's important is how people handle them, whether one has the will to make the wish a reality."

"You think I'm just daydreaming, don't you?" She smiled, inviting comment.

"Exactly," I continued. "If you act out wishes, that's one thing. If you don't—well, what would you call it—escapism?"

"I see myself getting stuck in a rut. I've thought about pulling up stakes and going to another city. There's no way of doing anything about dress designing here. It means giving up the earning power I have, leaving family ties. It seems so formidable. What do you think?"

I told her that so far it sounded as if she had made a better case for *not* changing fields. If she had to ask others for advice, then perhaps she wasn't sure enough in her own mind about making such a drastic change.

I was thinking how different she was—rational and sensible—from a good many others I've seen and listened to. There are people who are perennial daydreamers. I am still awed by the astronomical number of wishful thoughts, ingenious ideas, and dreams that people struggle to make a reality: teachers who want to be film makers, accountants scouting to invest in ski lodges or travel agencies, pharmacists trying to cultivate hydroponic gardens. At the very least, bringing your wishes out in the open gives you a little extra insight into the man or woman within. But to make them materialize means going beyond dreams and even insights. It means doing something about them.

"I guess you have to be careful with other people's careers," Carole said as we were leaving.

"Just as cautious as you are with other people's money," I replied. And on that note we parted.

I wished that I could make everyone realize that career decisions are personal decisions: fulfilling them depends on your readiness to act.

To thine own self be true

There's an attorney in California who appears in court wearing blue jeans and a Chamber of Commerce executive in Washington, D.C., who teaches a university seminar on the history of modern revolutions. In Providence, Rhode Island, an insurance agent coaches the college tennis team. A personnel director in Mobile, Alabama, keeps his hair at shoulder length.

Self-expression is in style again. More people are finding more ways to make their work styles match their life styles. People have always found outlets for their individuality, but today you can practice your convictions more freely. Modes and mores are being questioned, and prejudice is being routed. People are bursting out of confining roles and acting out the images they have of themselves.

Like it or not, there's a new kind of thinking. "I'm not just a bookkeeper [or a manager or a salesman]. I'm a person." If that's not a new attitude, it's a newly expressed attitude. People are speaking their minds at last!

Attitudes towards work are changing, too. Minds are stretching; imaginations are stirring; and independent thinking is respected.

You, too, can declare your independence. If you'd like to raise dogs, Irish bread, or a political issue, now is your chance.

Even the system is being humanized. Words like *relevant* and *involved* are creeping into the vocabulary of chairmen of the board. Management is beginning to respond to employees' needs for rewards other than a paycheck—needs to achieve and to be recognized for that achievement.

Employees at all levels are assuming more responsibility and participation in decision-making. In an ever-increasing number of corporations—lumber, food, and electronics—workers help run the show. It makes good business sense to encourage everyone to know and care about what's going on. For employees, it means greater job satisfaction; for employers, it means a more stable staff. Both benefit.

Finally, after years of disregarding inequality, management has begun to initiate programs to combat discrimination in hiring practices. Affirmative Action Programs are being adopted every day, thanks to the combination of legislation, government pressure, and the initiative of minority groups themselves.

If your goal is a step in a new direction, it takes more than a wish to make it happen. Freedom of choice is often expensive. Making waves instead of being caught in the current means that you must have the strength of your convictions. Making impossible dreams possible begins with that same look at your traits and characteristics, your aims and priorities. Decide how far they will take you. *If you don't serve your own self-interest, who will?* If you care enough about your career, do what you must, or you'll be looking for a job over and over again.

Michael Orcino is a case in point. He first thought about his career goals when he started looking for his first job. After all, growing into adulthood is enough to keep you busy without trying to map out your whole life. Few, even those with professional training, know at the outset just how their careers will unfold. Often, perhaps too often, careers are the result of chance.

Michael had no particular scenario to follow, but, being somewhat introspective, he had the good sense to get to know himself just about as well as any of us can.

20

In college he majored in American studies because he liked the subject. He rejected family pressures to become a lawyer, and his talents in art were yet undeveloped. True, he built the scenery for the senior play and wrote the lyrics for a school musical, but these were just hobbies.

Typically, he got his first job by default. The summer after graduation a friend of his went to work as a trainee for the Ace Greeting Card Company. In late August the friend got word of his acceptance in medical school and arranged for Michael to be interviewed by his boss. As a result, Michael's first job was writing get-well doggerel. Six months later he was promoted to Birthdays. Next, he was put in charge of Christmas. About this time he married Betty, the resident poet in Anniversaries. The two of them wrote—and learned about running a business. Within five years they bought the company outright, but administrative problems, sales promotion gimmicks, and personnel crises were a never ending rat race.

There never seemed to be time to go to the theater or to an art exhibit. For Michael, it was a struggle to pursue his special hobby, sculpture.

"Is that all there is?" he found himself asking.

"Money, yes; but time to enjoy it, no," he found himself answering. And in time the desire to accomplish something personally rewarding became an overwhelming motivation for a drastic change. It took a great deal of soul-searching to realize what mattered and to follow his star, but he did.

After a while he freely admitted to himself and to Betty his deep need to be a sculptor. The talent was there, he felt, and sculpting was the one thing that would be completely fulfilling. He began to take action to fulfill his dream. It took two years to sell the greeting card business. Then Michael began formal training in art, and Betty, who was somewhat of a gourmet cook, became an apprentice to a French chef, with the hope of opening a restaurant.

Epilogue: They bought a restaurant in a resort town. It's open for business six months a year and sculpture headquarters the other six months.

There is no guarantee that everybody's ambition will be fulfilled quite that completely. Even with thorough planning, purposefulness, and patience, circumstances can seem to conspire to keep goals from being realized.

For example, I know a politician who resigned from his county job in order to do what he felt was more honest work. For years his hobby had been tinkering in the lab he had set up in his basement. Whenever we met, he would tell me he was on the brink of some discovery or ready to patent a revolutionary formula. Well, he finally did make a breakthrough!

He developed a way to clean the exterior of buildings with chemicals instead of the conventional air-blasting method. His claim that his formula was more efficient and economical was well documented. Unfortunately, he was never able to raise enough money to put together a marketing organization for his new product.

Where is he now? He's a hospital administrator. Yet after hours he spends time in the lab, testing and experimenting. For him, the *striving* for fulfillment became its own reward.

To have the courage of your convictions, I believe, adds meaning to whatever you do. Dreams come true for a very few, as they did for Michael and Betty, but we all should treat the belief we have in ourselves with tender loving care.

Putting your ideal to work in the real world

" 'Sorry, but I'm going to have to let you go.' Those were my boss's very words to me. It was one of the happiest moments of my life," recalled Vincent Wycks. "I gave that louse eleven years of my life. I took his crummy little mom-and-pop trucking business and built an interstate organization. Me. By myself. Chief estimator. And he turned around and sold a two-million-dollar business to a conglomerate. What's more—in the new operation a computer has my job!"

That was the first day of the rest of Vince's life. "I had some money in the bank, more than enough to cover my bills," he said. "Now was the time to do what I wanted. Go back to my first love."

Vince had stayed on at Iowa State after graduation as an announcer for WHIS for a year or so. That job was his first love, but due to budget cuts, it ended all too soon. Now, after a good many years, he wanted to return to radio.

Instinctively he had the good sense to contact old cronies who promised to try to help (always a good idea; even if they don't have jobs in their pockets, their advice, suggestions, and interest are

22

valuable). At the same time, Vince blanketed a hundred-mile radius with his résumé and tapes and applied for a training position at a radio station. Not unexpectedly, he was turned down for that job—thirty-six-year-olds are hardly ever considered beginners.

"Would you go back to what you were doing?" I asked.

"What are you—crazy? I wouldn't be an estimator if it—"

"I don't mean estimating. But if you transfer your sales ability to the airwaves, it might be the best way to solve your problem. Call it a compromise. It's a combination of putting what you can do to work where you want to be. I'm suggesting the possibility of applying for a position in radio time sales, selling time to advertisers."

"What you're telling me is that I can't fulfill my goal overnight, that I'm stuck with selling until I add a new string to my bow," Vince said, somewhat deflated.

"That's it," I replied. "The very meaning of *career* implies life-long work, not instant achievement."

But today some people are restless. They are not willing to wait a lifetime for careers to mature. Consider the new work ethic. It's the old Puritan ethic recycled. Ambition and hard work are directed toward achieving inner gratification first and only then corporate accomplishments.

People are more selective about the types of organizations they want to be identified with, the kinds of groups they relate to, and the purpose of the work they perform. They are more concerned about company functions and objectives than they are about working hours and pension plans. They want meaningful occupations, not just income-producing work.

For example, an awakened social conscience has stirred some attorneys from their paneled offices to contribute time and talent to legal aid programs. Physicians participate in public health projects. Educators develop innovative methods to teach less advantaged students. Many scientists from every discipline take a humanistic approach to technology.

Today, technological progress is being defined in terms of societal gains. Putting contraptions on automobile exhaust pipes to control the emission of fumes is good. But if those very gadgets produce more dangerous poisons, that's bad. Many corporations are becoming more responsive to the need to conduct their business in the public interest. Human resources are being harnessed to improve the human condition.

Yet sometimes people who want jobs that will involve them in

23

helping others can't find them. This may be because they want to help others before they help themselves.

Look to your own background for achievements that can be signposts toward future endeavor. You'll find that almost all of them—dorm president, organizer of student voter registration, head of the tutorial service—were the result of knowledge and expertise acquired gradually. Didn't you have to prove yourself and demonstrate your capability before you were given responsibility for coordinating a project or setting its policy?

Ann Delford doggedly pursued positions in social service fields. She majored in sociology at Bryn Mawr and was willing to consider any job opportunity as long as it wasn't secretarial. But when she applied for a position with a health organization on the advice of a friend (not even the best advice from our best friends can be expected to produce results all the time), it turned out to be just clerical. And when she was interviewed at a local drug abuse council in response to an ad in the paper, all they wanted was a typist. Ann kept asking herself, "Doesn't a college degree mean anything?"

"Well, it's like this," I told Ann. "No one is going to hire you to be in charge of anything until you know enough about something."

"All I'm ever asked is 'Do you type?' It drives me up the wall. Men aren't asked how fast they type. Why do they ask us? I don't think I had to spend four years in college to be a secretary."

"A lot of women who are administrators, researchers, and editors began their careers behind a typewriter," I told her.

"Oh no! Are you one, too? Are you telling me that's the only job I can get? Has using one's mind gone out of style?"

"Relax a minute. The type of job you get depends on what you bring to the position. Math majors work with figures—quantitatively or theoretically. Chemists get their basic training in a lab. But a B.A. in sociology doesn't make you a sociologist—regardless, incidentally, of whether you're a she or a he."

"But men do get offered career jobs, while women—"

"Sure, if you're an engineer, an architect, or a dentist, you get a career job. Let's keep sex out of this."

"I refuse to do manual labor. Ten tapping fingers on a typewriter! It's the last thing I'll do!"

"The first thing you should do is stop griping so much. I'm with you. The best insurance against a routine job is being able to offer specific talents beyond being bright and willing."

"If I had a decent job, I could continue my education. I'd probably go to law school."

"OK. Let's be practical. If you're lucky, you can find an ordinary job that grows as you do, one that promises to improve if you do, too."

"Yes, Mrs. Taylor, you look as if you're ready to tell me about some dull office job. No thanks. I hate to keep reminding you that men are not forced into those roles."

"Really? Where have you been? If they have no special training, they're hired for jobs in 'public relations'—a euphemism for sales—or as 'management trainees'—clerical workers in disguise. Their lot is not a happy one, though I will say they complain less and do more to get ahead as quickly as possible."

"This has been a waste of time. I'm no nearer to a good job than before I came."

"I'm not so sure about that. Either you'll make something of a nothing job or you'll get further training."

She did both. Ann went to work for a criminal lawyer, typing briefs. It was not a challenging job, but with her salary she could afford to continue learning. She studied at night to become a paralegal professional. In time she was able to combine her sociological training with her legal aid work. The biggest surprise of all was that she used both fields to open the door to interests in documentation, computers, and systems analysis.

You may recognize the name of Dr. Margaret Drilling. Recently she declined a presidential nomination to the board of directors of the National Science Foundation, although years ago to be in government service would have meant the fulfillment of her ideal.

In her early life, as a young chemist, Margaret had applied for a position in the Department of Agriculture. In those days their laboratory facilities were far more sophisticated than any in her home state and represented an awesome challenge.

Her search for a government job began with filling out lengthy forms, giving them the same kind of attention to detail she would have applied to a scientific experiment. She gave sensible answers to silly questions and carefully documented information about the minutiae of her life—past and present. Why not? Rules are rules, and if that's what they wanted her to do, that's what she wanted to do. She took the Federal Service Entrance Examination and completed it with ease. After all, what else would you expect from a *magna cum laude?*

Then she waited for word. And waited. Finally she received her government rating—GS 7—a sort of hunting license certifying her eligibility to work for Uncle Sam. So she was cleared and ready to hunt for a government job. She arrived in Washington in January hoping to begin the new year with a new job. But she got tangled immediately in the web of bureaucratic red tape.

Those who interviewed her were very impressed, they said. They would hire her today, they said—*if* they had a slot, or *if* the budget is approved, or *if* the appropriation is made, or *if* new legislation is passed.

Her search lengthened into a full-fledged campaign. You might say she occupied Washington, trying to plow through the departmental maze. But in the end Washington did not offer an occupation to Margaret. Her search had been in vain. It was the wrong time and the wrong place, as often happens.

She departed with mixed emotions to accept a position with a pharmaceutical company. Through the years, she distinguished herself for her research in serology. Pioneering a breakthrough in the storage of blood platelets was just one of her achievements.

News of her nomination to the National Science Foundation Board reached her at the university laboratory. As head of a research team experimenting with vaccines, she felt strongly committed to the project as well as to her graduate students, and so she declined the honor. Recognition from the government was gratifying, but not nearly so important now as it would have been in the form of an entry-level job twenty years earlier. She had accomplished far more than the goal she had set for herself at that time.

Ideals change, just as people do. Margaret was no longer the person who wished for a government job; therefore, when she finally was offered one, it no longer mattered.

I had never met the man who telephoned, asking me to be patient as he explained his problem. He wanted to know whether I could help him find an overseas position. He said he was a mathematician for a telecommunications firm that was relocating to Ohio. That was not exactly his idea of the garden spot of the world, he said, and if he had to move he'd really prefer to go abroad.

Well, I said, many companies do hire people for overseas positions, but he should be aware that it is a complicated process and sometimes difficult to negotiate. Reluctantly, he came to the same conclusion as his efforts in search of a job overseas bore no fruit.

So he followed his firm to Ohio. As a result of expansion, he was given special training for a new computer operation. This in turn gave him the very capability he needed to qualify for a position in the company's Melbourne office. I learned of this development quite by accident when his company was searching for his replacement, and I think of it whenever I meet a person who expects instant fulfillment of job goals.

Just as job seekers have great expectations for jobs they want to find, so have employers great expectations of employees they want to hire. Job seekers have no monopoly on being unrealistic; personnel managers are just as guilty. Whether they're looking for a CPA to handle internal audits, or a Ph.D. to design questionnaires, or a secretary to take dictation from four sales representatives, they would also like employees who are brilliant, charming, dynamic, attractive, witty, and sophisticated.

"We want a man," they will tell me, "with a background in engineering and finance, five years of experience in utilities, and capable of managing a research division. Salary, about twenty thousand."

If you had a Geiger counter or a divining rod, chances are you couldn't discover a person in the whole country who had those qualifications and would be willing to work at that price.

Three months later, who do they offer the job to? An engineer with three years of utilities experience and no financial background. His starting salary is twenty-two thousand and he agrees to take courses in money and banking. This is a sensible selection and a realistic solution.

I approve of formulating an ideal as a point of departure, but only as an incentive to find the best employee or the best job. Then reality and practicality should take over. The job you do accept, imperfect though it may be, has the potential to improve. And the employee who is hired, imperfect though he may be, has that same potential.

Getting from where you are to where you want to be

Happiness is being able to say "I like my job." That's the consensus of dozens of personnel managers who have shared their professional views with me. Personnel managers are sensitive to many nuances of career development; even so, their guidance is likely to be general. You must adapt their advice for your own personal use. In the final analysis *you* must prescribe for yourself.

Once I had a long interview with a photographer, Arthur Pendleton, who was on the staff of a metropolitan daily. The newspaper's personnel manager had suggested that Arthur see me. The paper was about to merge with its competitor, and Arthur was considering all his options.

We discussed various possibilities, from continuing to do the same work in the new setup to going into his own business. Arthur felt his advancement would be stymied in the changing organization; yet a business venture of his own seemed quite risky.

We considered commercial art as an alternative, for he had talent in that direction. But starting over in a new field would mean not only a salary cut but returning to a low-man-on-the-totem-pole status. It's sometimes very difficult, after earning the respect of your peers and exercising considerable responsibility, to find suddenly that you're a novice again. Arthur expressed an interest in teaching but realized that this would be contingent upon further education, which was not possible at the time.

It's uncanny how many twists and turns a career might take. I remember asking him whether he had any desire to get into management of a newspaper. The question triggered an unexpected response. Arthur seemed to be thinking out loud and admitted that his work really hadn't been satisfying lately. He didn't like the pace, the hustling, or the hours.

"There are so many problem situations I see in which I can just picture a solution," Arthur rambled on. "The other day I was caught in a traffic jam, and it was so easy for me to visualize how, with re-routing, these snarls could be corrected." This comment gave me a clue. Arthur had a knack for conceptualizing abstractions. I went back to his earlier remarks about art, and he showed me some samples of a group of cartoon characters who voiced his own point of view.

In time I was able to bring his work to the attention of a northeastern chain of newspapers. They offered him a job as cartoonist/photographer. Arthur accepted the job because it was the closest he could get at present to doing what he wanted to do.

Before you can decide what job you want, you must ask yourself, "What can I do *now?*" This logical approach was recommended by a gentleman with many years of experience in the personnel field. "And be damned honest," he urged. "Review your assets, experience, and background. What you have done in the past will largely determine what you can do in the future. Your opportunities will depend on what you bring to a job. But be candid about your liabilities as well. Do you have the necessary preparation for the job you want? Have you the innate capability to achieve your goal? And will you pursue it with determination?"

A reporter told me recently that he didn't want to be a newspaperman for the rest of his life, although he was highly regarded in his field. After nine years in journalism his skill was razor sharp. He talked about essays and mused about the short stories he hoped to write someday. But he never got beyond the talking stage, for he had made no effort to develop a style for the kind of writing he wanted to do.

Certain goals require a great deal of discipline. If self-discipline is not your forte, then give up that particular goal; it's only a figment of your daydreams.

"Saying one thing and doing another is a common failing," comments the head of personnel of a non-profit organization. "As a matter of fact, we in the personnel field are just as guilty as the job seeker. I can't tell you how many times we have talked one way and acted another."

Pressed for specifics, he told me that his company's work in environmental research had interested many people who were anxious to work for the organization on any level. "We say we won't hire an overqualified applicant for a junior position, but we do. Then we've got, say, an economist with more skills than we need who has a job with less challenge than she wants. It's a two-way street. The person must fit the job, and the job must fit the person."

Other practical advice comes from an outspoken director of personnel. "People are too emotional about finding a job," he said. "Why don't they use reason? Sometimes they do the most inconceivable things. For example, right now I need a statistician. I interviewed a very competent applicant and offered him the position. He turned it down. Why? He didn't want to be a statistician, he said. Well, that was a jolt! Here's a man applying for a job as a statistician who doesn't want to be a statistician. I ask you, does that add up?"

"I think people can learn a great deal about themselves from the things they don't want to do and the jobs they don't like," I said to Security National Bank's director of personnel, Roger Lyons.

"Yes, I agree," Lyons replied. "Provided they take the time to analyze the factors involved. All I ask is that they think clearly. Either a man understands what it is he doesn't like about his work and why he thinks he'd like different work, or his search for job satisfaction will be in vain."

There are many considerations in selecting a career beyond the kind of work you do and what it pays. As Edward Shannon, personnel manager of General Documentation, put it, "You're off to a good start once you set to rest the things you can't do or won't do. That in itself can teach you a lesson and even shed some light on possible job problems."

"Once people stop trying to be what they're not, all sorts of possibilities surface," I added. "It's amazing how many real opportunities remain even after your fantasies are shattered."

We agreed that more mobility exists within a given field than between fields. Progressive experience in a single specialization opens the door to variations on the same theme.

Ed Shannon offered his very own background as proof of the point we were discussing. He described himself as a generalist, experienced in recruiting, employee relations, and training.

"I'm on the prowl myself," he confided to me. "I don't expect to be with General Documentation forever. I'm looking around."

"What kind of position would you be receptive to?"

"First let me tell you what I'm not looking for—the usual PR job. I'm not creative. Nor a job in education. Although there's a tie-in between education and personnel training, that's not the route I'm interested in following. I have a number of choices."

I realized that Ed was about to give a demonstration of instant self-analysis, and he did. "I could use my employee relations experience as a door-opener to labor relations," he said, "or get some wage and salary exposure by going into an industrial research department and adding a new skill to my repertoire. Another possibility is to continue as a generalist but go with a larger organization. On balance, I think it's more advantageous to specialize. Then you always have something concrete to offer. But regardless of where I go there are many other things to consider. I'd rather remain in the suburbs instead of doing daily battle with downtown traffic. I want to be able to respect the man I work for and be given a reasonable amount of independence. Does that tell you enough?"

"It tells me you've given a good deal of thought to your future," I answered. "Of course, this is what I'd expect of a personnel man—realistic and clearly defined aims."

"One mistake people make," Ed continued, "is thinking they should change fields when the job seems a dead end or the salary inadequate or the boss impossible. With a little imagination and resourcefulness, they can promote their know-how to a higher level of responsibility."

"Don't look for your next job," cautions Frank Durante, employment manager of an insurance company, "unless you really want to make a change. Sure, you can go on interview after interview, learn something about the decor of many different offices, have chit-chats with friendly folks; but unless you're ready to act, you're only spinning your wheels."

Everybody likes to get into the act when it comes to giving career advice. Whether or not you accept their good counsel depends to some degree on your opinion of the adviser.

Over the years I have heard many comments about counselors—both college vocational counselors and employment counselors. They seem not to have distinguished themselves in the public's mind. Generally, the former are considered naive and the latter unprofessional.

The director of personnel of a utility company lamented that "vocational guidance counselors seem to have no notion of what employers expect of employees. Misguidance is worse than no guidance."

Applicants have regaled me with "A plague on both your houses." For every complaint that a college counselor's advice was impractical and misinformed, there is a criticism that an employment counselor misrepresented a job or was only interested in getting a fee.

I urge all guidance counselors to leave the sanctity of the cloistered campus long enough to find out what really happens in the market place. And I urge all employment counselors to go back to the classrooms for training in business theory, industrial relations, and psychology.

Employers too must share some responsibility for shaping careers. They have an obligation to put an end to discriminatory practices, to attempt to reduce boring routine, to be receptive to constructive suggestions. Indeed, management must create a climate in which an employee can work at what he was hired to do.

If someone is charged with certain responsibility, he must also be given the authority to carry it out. And if a training program is offered, it must be a bona fide one—not just a job title but an organized learning experience. For management to do less is to waste talent and to visit indignity on men and women who offer unplumbed abilities.

Finally, getting from where you are now to where you want to be involves being prepared when opportunity knocks.

Most personnel managers agree that careers improve with time and with the efforts you put into your own advancement. If you want to be a department head, familiarize yourself with every function in the department and notice how good managers deal with people. Participation in policy-making requires not only good judgment but knowledge of industry at large and the forecasts for its future.

These are the initiatives that promote careers. In turn, I feel it's an important part of personnel policy to reward those who have shown these initiatives with career promotions. What can be more important in the realm of employment than being able to say, "I like my job," and hearing your employer tell you, "I like the job you're doing"?

PART 2: YOUR MARKETABILITY IN THE JOB MARKET

What you should know before someone will hire you

You need to know only three things in order to get a job:

1. What you have to offer.
2. Who needs it.
3. How to make them want it.

But the most important thing of all is to be able to perceive the relationship between your experience and employers' requirements. This link brings together employers who have jobs to fill and people who have skills that fit the jobs.

In this section we'll go through the three points listed above, studying the best techniques for bringing your talents to the attention of the right employer.

The strategy is modeled on a market research program. If you develop such a program, you can be certain that your objectives will be achieved with greater efficiency in terms of time, effort and money. What's more, you'll make a better, informed final decision.

Marketing is a system of action. The first step is to diagnose the problem by means of what the pros call an *audit*. The second is to gather information—*data collection*. And the third is to develop and execute your approach by what is known in the trade as *effective action*.

Let's have a close look at each of these procedures. They will demonstrate how the job search theories discussed thus far are practiced in real life.

The audit: self-assessment

Getting a job involves following the laws of supply and demand. It's a two-way process; something is sold and someone will buy.

"What am I—a tube of toothpaste?" a skeptical job seeker once asked me. "I'm just looking for a job. You're telling me I've got to advertise myself as if I were a product. Merchandise myself like a commodity. I've been an assistant in a purchasing department. What do you expect me to do—send out promotional material, go on radio, hire a high-powered advertising agency to create a TV commercial that will make my name a household word? All I want to do is work."

"Well," I said, "believe it or not, you're on the right track. You might as well learn the facts of life while there's still time. Yes, getting a job calls for some salesmanship."

As a job seeker, you must see yourself in this context: you perform a service; it is valuable and therefore salable; and you can put it on the market to attract a buyer.

As a seller, you must know your product, identify its uses, create interest, stimulate demand, and make the sale.

Here's how. The service you offer is unique, for there is only one you. That thought alone should be an ego-boost that will build your confidence and help you project your self-image.

Know thy self-image intimately. That's the first thing you must learn in your role of salesperson. Technically, it's called *product identification.*

Most people have some general career plan based, to a degree, on knowledge derived from self-evaluation. They take a mental inventory of their abilities and decide how and where they would like to invest them. But it is a rare person who manages his or her career flawlessly. One such person is a man named Charles Wright.

The other day he called. "It was a tough decision," he said, "but I turned down the company's offer to send me overseas."

"Chuck, everyone should have the luxury of your kind of tough decisions," I told him.

Ten years ago Charles Wright came to me for employment counseling. He told me candidly that he could get a job without my help, but he wanted some career information. From then on our acquaintance has thrived on mutual respect. We hardly ever see each other, but we keep in touch. Whenever Charles is about to take another step up the career ladder we analyze his options.

We first met when Charles graduated from Rutgers.

"I want to learn a thing or two before I go to work," he told me. (That's a refreshing attitude in my business!)

Charles explained that he had been recruited on campus by one of the Big Eight accounting firms, Pace Witthouse, and before he gave them a final answer he wanted to do some comparison shopping.

"You must be good," I told him. "That's quite a distinction."

But he didn't need me to corroborate that fact; he had a healthy supply of self-confidence and with good reason. To his credit already were a full four-year scholarship and honors in his double major of economics and accounting. He even found time to be business manager of the campus newspaper and captain of the hockey team.

I think the things that impressed me most were that he knew where he was going, he had the drive to get there and the innate resourcefulness to find the way.

"I want to be a corporate executive someday," he told me confidently. "I'm aware that your basic first job is like serving an apprenticeship. You only get an overview of the scope of business problems. If you're lucky, you're given responsibility. I don't want to be lucky—I want to make it happen."

"So what do you want to know? Which company will give you the best training, let you work independently, promote you quickly, and 'look good on a résumé?' "

"I don't quite know whether you're being facetious or serious," he said, looking serious himself, "but OK, let's say those are my primary concerns. At the moment, I want to get off to a good start. Working independently can wait. Getting promoted will depend on my own growth. And I guess I'm enough of a snob to want to work for a prestigious firm."

Well, he was honest about it—the *kind* of firm he wanted to be associated with mattered. "You've just solved your own problem. Accept the job offer with Pace Witthouse. It answers your present objectives," I advised him.

"Thanks for listening. And thanks for not trying to talk me into a job just so you'd get a fee."

Charles called occasionally, sometimes just to tell me about a job-seeking friend he was referring to me. About two years later we got together for another strategy session. He told me he thought he was at the crossroads and had to make a choice.

"We both know I can't go much further at Pace Witthouse without my CPA. Of course, I'd be in the same spot if I switched to another accounting firm. My problem is that I don't think I want to specialize in accounting for the rest of my life, and yet I don't think I'm ready to move to a major corporation."

"What about a minor corporation?" I asked. "No, seriously, let's look at this objectively. Getting ahead depends on your ability to perform at a higher level. If it's not going to be the accounting route, what will make you a more attractive candidate to a blue-chip firm?"

We agreed that getting his M.B.A. would add the extra values and bring Charles closer to his ultimate goal of corporate management.

This game plan worked out especially well. The timing was ideal; the fact that Charles began his graduate studies at a time when he was completely adjusted to his job at Pace Witthouse meant that he could handle both without stress. As I recall, it was at about that time that I got an announcement of his marriage. Obviously *all* was going well.

Charles wrote to tell me that his courses in taxation had made it possible for him to analyze the foreign income tax structure of a client (Jersey Stanco) and that the report he wrote had come to the attention of the company's executive committee. Soon he began working closely with Jersey Stanco's finance department on tax problems and ultimately was invited to join their staff. He had no hesitation about accepting the job. He had gotten to know some of the people in the department and found them very compatible. And he felt he was now heading in the right direction.

I sent a letter of congratulations to Charles and made a mental note to watch his progress, for I was certain that his future career would be something to watch!

When I saw him recently, Charles looked the picture of success. He had matured, and maturity had made him more handsome. That day, I got quite a lesson in executive upward mobility. It was fascinating to observe it across the table as Charles sketched the highlights of his climb toward the executive suite.

"I'm very grateful for the opportunities that have come my way," he said, but his modesty was transparent. "That I have used them to full advantage, I attribute to a number of things. High on the list would be the fact that I know who I am and what I'm good at. Believe me, it makes getting where you want to go a hell of a lot easier." He sipped his Bloody Mary.

"In the past few years my special forte has been my analytical ability. Also, I like administrative work and I find I can communicate with all levels of management."

Then he went into some details about his career. After specializing in tax analysis he had moved into the treasurer's office, where he had assisted and advised in matters related to budgets and acquisitions. He had just completed a study of least-cost multi-country financing techniques, and as a result the corporation was offering him an overseas assignment.

"A very tempting offer, indeed, but then a more tempting one came along. You know, I've always felt that if you want to get ahead you've got to see beyond your own company. You've got to take a broad view of the entire industry. You know I've had my antenna up for a spot in corporate management."

"Chuck, I think I know what happened. You've probably carefully cultivated some excellent contacts through the years, and at the right moment you were remembered. Tell me, who's the fortunate company, and what will you be doing?"

"I'm going with Inter-Continental Oil as assistant director of international finance."

"Someday you'll be president of an oil company," I said, and meant it. "Men with your drive and single-mindedness, who know how to manage their time and energy and can motivate others, usually make it to the top."

He just smiled casually. But we both knew.

As I walked back to my office, I couldn't help but think how infrequently people control their destiny and how frequently destiny controls people.

Most of us surely remember with a shudder what happened in late 1973. We don't know the end of the story yet, but we do know the beginning. You couldn't pick up the morning paper without seeing headlines like:

> 25,000 Airline Employees Laid Off
> Area Gas Stations Fold
> Truckers Stage Strike Against Impact of Energy Crisis on Profits
> Housing Industry Feeling Effects of Energy Restrictions
> Fuel Pinch: Will It Be Squeezing the Arts?
> Asphalt, Plastic, Chemical Products Feel Effects of Energy Crunch
> Oil Crisis Sends Stock Prices Sliding
> Search for Offshore Oil Quickens

In this decade alone, engineers and technicians have suddenly found themselves unemployed as a result of cutbacks in the space program. Educators have unexpectedly found themselves out of work due to shrinking school enrollments. Even the printing industry, whose members are strongly organized, is suffering from technological changes. The disruptive effects of these trends have taken their toll on large segments of the labor force.

The domino theory is operative here. Engineers and computer analysts who lose their jobs trigger a slowdown in the economy that affects accountants, marketing specialists, secretaries, and salesmen. Dehiring seems to be the order of the day, and the next, and the next.

Dehiring has many aliases. The government calls it an RIF (reduction in force); the airlines call it a furlough; the auto industry, a layoff; some call it termination. But the result is the same—you're out of work.

Now circumstances are putting you to the test. Are your inner resources, imagination, knowledge of the market place, and understanding of your own marketability equal to the times? Do you see the opportunity that lurks hidden in the crisis?

Recently, perhaps because these economic crises seem to be occurring more frequently, management has made a concerted effort to reposition employees whose jobs suddenly end for economic reasons. When possible, persons are transferred to other departments. It's become common practice for a boss to check out possible positions for his staff with other companies. Companies organize workshops and seminars in job search techniques to assist affected employees. Occasionally they hire professional search firms to expedite the placement of terminated personnel. If feasible, they may extend severance pay and fringe benefits.

Yet basically, the responsibility for weathering the rough times is *yours.* I have counseled hundreds of people in this predicament, and there are hundreds of solutions to the problem.

During the recent energy crunch I made a survey of employees furloughed by the airlines. You don't have to be a pilot or a stewardess to understand the dilemma. The ways they found to meet the situation can be helpful to anyone who is unemployed involuntarily, and the diversity of the solutions is offered as evidence that you needn't be a victim of circumstance.

Elizabeth Ziese was furloughed just when she was due for a promotion. She wasn't going to allow herself to be an unemployment statistic. She had come too far and worked too hard. Beth had the good sense to realize that even in a tight employment market good people are still in great demand. More than ever, management must employ the most qualified people, for business survival depends on them.

Beth had learned to be a valuable employee early in her career. Even as a computer operator trainee she was aware that employers wanted the best people they could hire as much as employees wanted the best job they could find, so she always tried to add *something* that was not required by her job description—something that would help make the operation more successful. That's why she continued her studies. She saw beyond the job she was performing and knew that her own future depended on her growth. Therefore, her promotion to programmer benefited both her and the company. Beth recognized her marketable assets—her understanding of the objectives and problems of the computer department, her ability to handle responsibility, her rapport with the people she supervised and with her own supervisor.

Beth was ready to turn crisis into opportunity. Though she had not thought of making a change voluntarily, she would use all the initiative she could summon now that a change was forced upon her. She promised herself a better job at a higher salary. I'll tell you how Beth transferred her skills from one payroll to another later on as we discuss the other aspects of marketability.

For Captain Chet Thomas it was a time to rethink his whole life style. At fifty-two, retirement was just over the horizon, and early retirement had a number of things to recommend it. In recent years two other events—a strike and a temporary lay-off—had stopped his salary. He had become increasingly uneasy about the uncertainty of his income. Drawing his pension regularly would provide at least a secure base. He figured he'd let the company pin silver wings on his chest for his twenty-five years of service, but he had had enough of the sky and was ready to return to the land. Those acres he'd bought some years ago seemed mighty attractive now, so he made plans to settle there and go into chicken farming. Thomas was one of the lucky ones who had a choice; all he needed was a little shove towards the next phase of his life.

Then there was Eileen Johnson, one of four in ground crew security who were furloughed. She'd been with the airlines for less than a year, and this was the first time she had gone through such an experience. At the beginning of the crisis her boss told her he thought her job was safe, so she didn't worry. Even when the newspapers, radio, and TV started to give a grimmer and grimmer picture of the immediate future of the economy, Eileen remained calm. Then one day she was let go. Still, she didn't panic. Because the company continued her flight privileges, she visited her family for a while. When she returned she called her former employer to explore the possibility of being rehired. No chance. She applied for several positions, but, she told me later, she thought she was suspect, for prospective employers would think she'd leave should the airline recall her. She waited a month for a job in a hotel to materialize, but it never did.

Ninety days without an income had nearly depleted her financial resources, yet when Eileen came to see me she managed to keep her cool. I was not about to inject a note of anxiety if she had none. I made two suggestions. One was the buddy system: pooling information about jobs that any of her furloughed colleagues developed. The rationale was that a job that didn't interest one might appeal to another. The second suggestion came from a newspaper article I had read. The FBI had announced that for the first time in its history it would accept women for positions as special agents. It seemed to me Eileen's background in security in the ground crew might be considered useful experience. The idea pleased her. It took another four months before she was appointed, and during the entire waiting period she was without work.

There's really no moral to this story. It's just one example of how one person confronted her problem. Her easygoing nature helped prevent undue stress. Oh, maybe for the duration she had to give up buying clothes, taking taxis, and seeing movies. But she worked it out her own way.

But if you've just bought a house, as Jim Hobart had, and your wife is pregnant, and you've got no job, you've really got to hustle. When Jim, a former captain in the Air Force and a Vietnam veteran, received the news that his job as navigator had been eliminated, he went into a tailspin. Flying was the only way he had ever earned a paycheck. Who would pay him now and for what?

He responded to the emergency by switching to reflex action. Compulsively he studied the Help Wanted columns from A to Z. Impulsively he applied for jobs in public relations, administration, and management. He was so preoccupied with the urgent need to get a job that he never took a moment to consider his own strongest assets, the type of work he preferred to do, current market trends, or even his basic requirements for employment. Without ever properly identifying and analyzing his problem, he had no hope of finding his way to a job. He was getting nowhere fast, like an aircraft in a holding pattern.

Before long his emotions began to fray, his wife became nervous, the kids got cranky. Naturally. This lack of work was a creeping deflation of everyone's sense of well-being. How I was able to get Hobart on the right track is the subject of discussion further on in this section.

So far I have discussed two types of problems that turn employees into job seekers: the drive for upward mobility and the involuntary loss of a job. There is one other motivation for job change: dissatisfaction with one's present position.

I remember an office manager of a law firm who told me that she felt as though she were on a treadmill, plodding through the same old routine month after month. She found the bookkeeping duties dull, ordering supplies tedious, handling minor personnel problems a bore. She told me she had applied for other managerial positions, but none really seemed to be an improvement over the job she had.

"It's getting so that I can hardly drag myself to the office in the morning," Mary Capra admitted.

"You've got such a negative attitude," I told her, "that if a good opportunity came along and knocked you over, you'd probably say 'quit shoving.' I'd prescribe motivation shots if there were such a thing. Too bad. Working shouldn't be a grim experience, you know. You deserve your share of satisfaction."

"I thought I might try something different—like social work," she said.

"Have you any related experience?"

"Well, I was a phys ed major in college—that was a while back."

"I think you'll agree that's hardly adequate preparation for the field. But you probably could get a job in an administrative capacity with an organization engaged in some aspect of social work," I told her, trying to balance optimism with realism.

"But I want to get away from that," she reminded me. "I'm tired of shuffling papers. I want to do something that allows me to see the fruits of my labor. I want to enjoy what I'm doing and get a feeling of accomplishment."

"I'm all for that. Ideally, everyone should be employed in work they enjoy. Yet, you can't ignore the facts. Companies hire you for what you can do, not how you feel about it."

"That's my problem. I don't want to work at what I can do. I want to work at something I haven't done—without sacrificing income."

"But if you don't put previous experience to work in your next job, you're going to have to substitute something. What other talents do you have that might be developed?"

"Not too much, really, but I have been involved in several physical fitness programs on a volunteer basis. I've worked with youth groups at recreational centers. In the summer I give swimming instructions to handicapped children, and I help at the 'Y' with senior citizens' activities."

Could she employ these talents gainfully, or had she considered doing so at all? She had, but there was a problem: the type of position she qualified for would pay less than her current salary. As gently as I knew how, I pointed out that she could expect to be paid only what her contribution was worth to the employer. This did not go over too well. It never ceases to surprise me that some people expect to earn more at jobs for which they are less qualified!

I explained to Mary how she could build a career based on these alternate skills. Ultimately she might go into the field of physical or occupational therapy, perhaps even become a physician's assistant—a new and growing profession. Of course, additional training would be necessary. That didn't solve the immediate problem, but I suggested an interim plan to Mary. I advised her to explore job opportunities in the health field, applying for positions utilizing her present know-how. This new setting would be a bridge to the knowledge she was going to acquire. Then I asked her to compile a list of appropriate organizations and specific jobs for which she might apply. She agreed to keep me posted on her progress. She did—but more about it a little later on.

I am keenly aware of the many difficult job problems people

45

face. Each job seeker has a combination of problems peculiar to himself and his own circumstances. Yet experience proves that there are only a limited number of concrete solutions. Identifying the problem is the real problem; selecting a suitable solution is perhaps a little easier.

In Mary Capra's case the problems were that she was no longer happy with the type of work she was doing and she wanted to build a new career without sacrificing income. The suggested solutions were identifying and making use of alternate skills, then setting immediate goals as well as ultimate goals.

These same solutions apply to other situations. For example, a frustrated medical records supervisor may turn his abilities toward library work. A dissatisfied salesman might call on secondary experience and seek an advertising position in his own industry. A researcher might discover hidden talents in the art field, or a pension planner can redirect his experience into personnel benefits programs.

Almost anyone can regroup his assets and create a new version of himself or herself. But to accomplish that feat, each individual has to make a full audit—an inventory of all he has ever done or wanted to do.

Data collection: the Selectascope

The market researcher asks: How does the seller find out what the buyer wants? And how does he find out who the buyer is? Translated into job searchers' language: What are the job requirements? And which organization will hire me?

Job requirements and job qualifications are opposite sides of the same coin. Employers look at their requirements and your qualifications from their point of view. You see your qualifications and employers' requirements from your vantage point.

If you gather as much information as you possibly can about a job's requirements, you'll see the job more as the employer does, and you'll be better able to judge whether your qualifications are suitable. That's your first assignment in the data collection phase.

Your approach to information gathering will depend to some extent on whether you're job hunting to get ahead, or because you were unexpectedly forced into unemployment, or because you're dissatisfied with your present position. As a matter of fact, your reason for job hunting will probably influence your entire campaign, including your attitude toward it. Even the sources of information vary. Much useful information is easily available to employed job seekers who are looking to get ahead in their chosen careers.

For instance, it was very easy for Charles Wright, the would-be corporate executive, to plug in to a network of personnel news. He was right there on the scene where the action was. Not only was he privy to inside information, but, more important, he could judge its merit.

Among the many things you learn as your career develops is where power is and who has it. You get to know the prime movers in your field and to be known by them. These contacts are excellent sources of advice at job-change time.

Consciously and subconsciously the job seeker bent on upward mobility amasses a body of knowledge about his department, his organization, and the entire industry. He learns how management manipulates manpower and how people can affect the courses their careers can take. Knowing the internal operation of an organization means that you can better interpret the jobs that are to be filled.

For example, suppose Charles's company is looking for an assistant to the president. Charles, or anyone on the mid-level staff, obviously will understand the job better than will an outsider. He has the advantage of knowing the history of the job, the real reason for hiring, and the kind of person who would fit in the executive suite. Charles would know whether management was looking for someone who was well organized or whose work style was very imaginative. He would know the real requirements of the job, not just the stated ones.

This is valuable information for every job seeker. Those who cannot come by it easily will find that it pays to make the extra effort to get it.

Elizabeth Ziese, the ex-airline computer programmer, methodically organized the information she needed to reposition herself. She, too, had an established communications link to the computer world and therefore could deal with her job search more knowledgeably.

"What if I were going to hire myself?" Beth asked herself as if in an interview. What do you do best? Programming. Can you be more specific? I can write and debug programs in COBOL language for all financial data for the accounting department. Have you supervised others? Yes. Are you good at it? I think so. What other assets can you offer an employer? I've converted programs from one type of equipment to another. What about your other assets? I work well under pressure; I'm ambitious; I want to get ahead. Anything else? I want more money and job security; no more being out of a job due to circumstances beyond my control.

These answers became Beth's guideline for finding her job market. They helped her identify the type of work situation best suited to her background. She eliminated organizations that didn't meet her needs: consulting firms unable to give assurances of stability and security, small companies that could not offer the salary or advancement opportunity she desired. Then she eliminated companies whose requirements she could not meet: technical and scientific firms.

Beth prepared a list of types of businesses likely to hire her: utilities, banks, credit companies, accounting firms, and transportation businesses. She decided against utilities and transportation businesses because of the energy crisis. Banks and credit companies she rejected on the grounds that the work would not be diversified. Accounting firms, then, were the answer and met all of Beth's basic requirements. She opened the Yellow Pages to the listing of accountants. Starting with A, Beth went down the column, making calls to inquire about job openings. By her calculation, she figured she'd have a job before she was halfway through the alphabet. She was correct. Now she knows the joy of working.

Jim Hobart, the navigator, couldn't get his job search campaign off the ground.

When he came to see me he admitted that he had never worked harder in his life than he had during this period of unemployment. Jim told me what he had done in pursuit of a job.

"I must be doing something wrong; it doesn't seem possible to try so hard and not get hired." A crash course in vocational guidance was what he needed and what I gave him.

"There are forty thousand ways to make an honest living," I told him, "and damn it, we're going to pick one for you! Because you need to act quickly, I'm going to make a rash suggestion. Under these circumstances, use this rule of thumb—if you've never heard of a particular type of job, it's not for you."

"If I don't know what it is, I can't do it. That's what you're saying."

"Let's just say you can't get hired to do it as easily as you can get hired for something you *do* know about. And since you're anxious to go to work, let's confine ourselves to those things with which you are familiar."

"Does that include hobbies and interests?"

"Yes, of course, if they're marketable. What are yours?"

"Theater," Jim replied.

"If you weren't hurting for a job it might be worth exploring, but it's very risky for you to try to break into the theater professionally. I say for now it's not a good bet."

"So we get back to the question: What kinds of jobs do I compete for?"

"And which of your skills do you compete with?" I added.

"Remember, I'm trained for the aviation field. Period."

"Jim, either we've got to use that experience in an alternate way or come up with secondary abilities."

"I'm ready to do anything," Jim said in a tone of desperation.

"Not 'anything,' Jim. This is the very time to do something very special. Have you ever taken a battery of tests—abilities, aptitude, interest, or personality tests?"

"Oh, no! You're not going to suggest that. This is an emergency. Who needs shrinks now?"

"That's just the point. These tests are primarily for the purpose of vocational guidance. I've developed a questionnaire-survey for job guidance. I call it a Selectascope."

The Selectascope is a three-part self-help guide for assessing and correlating the job you can get and the job you can take. It outlines practical steps for a job seeker to take to meet the employer's job requirements as well as his own. It's especially useful for those who have to find a job quickly. The whole procedure can be completed in a week.

Here is the Selectascope. I asked Jim to give me his answers as soon as possible.

Part I Minimum Job Requirements
1. Salary.

2. Job functions.
3. Working conditions.
4. Benefits.
5. Location.
6. Other essentials.

Part II What Are Employers Looking For

This is a do-it-yourself survey. Choose a sample group of employers from occupations that are interesting to you, that you are knowledgeable about, or that are accessible to you.

1. Get reading materials.
2. Arrange a tour of a company (if possible).
3. Inquire about the nature of the work.
4. Learn about job functions.
5. Study job requirements.
6. Ask about recruitment policies.
7. Find out *why* employers hire the people they do.
   a. What they consider important.
   b. The qualifications they expect.

Let the experts in a given field counsel and advise you. The correlation between filling jobs and finding jobs suggests that you look to the people who fill jobs for the best clues to find jobs.

Part III What Have You Got That They Want?

Review your qualifications in terms of the information you gathered from your investigation into the field of your choice.

1. Most marketable skills.
2. Pertinent assets.
3. Related experience and achievements.
4. Appropriate abilities.
5. Aptitudes.
6. Interests.
7. Limitations.

Jim Hobart gave me his answers to Part I of the Selectascope the next morning.

1. Salary: $15,000.
2. Job functions: Planning the use and directing the operation of a mechanized activity.
3. Working conditions: Varied, changing, requiring physical energy, outdoors.
4. Benefits: Major medical.
5. Location: Within a fifty-mile radius of my home.
6. Other essentials: Opportunity for future advancement.

Several days later, I got a letter from Jim. He confessed that he had not had any intention of carrying out my suggestions and that the Selectascope questionnaire-survey had reminded him of his early school days. On the other hand, he hadn't anything better to do, so he had called an Air Force buddy who worked with a conglomerate to see whether he could be of any help. They had made arrangements to meet, and Jim had asked for a copy of the company's annual report.

He had been amazed at the scope of their operation. They provided food services to institutions, airlines, and colleges; maintained vending machines in plants, offices, and government buildings; and provided a linen supply service to industry.

Jim met with his friend, who introduced him to key division chiefs. They, in turn, made it possible for him to tour the purchasing department, mechanical shop, dispatcher's office, and computer room. He also met the head of the traffic department and asked about job functions, requirements, and what the department looked for in new employees.

He learned that 70 percent of the new employees came through word-of-mouth or employee referrals and that the company received over 300 unsolicited résumés a week and only gave serious consideration to a handful.

He also learned that applicants were evaluated differently by different people. For example, department chiefs were impressed

51

by specific skills and related experience, but personnel people seemed to be more concerned about motivation, attitude, and compatibility.

Jim and I put our heads together a few days later to sort out the facts.

"Jim, we know your job requirements. From the information you picked up, can you describe a job that meets those needs?"

"Working in a traffic department comes pretty close. There would be a good mix of duties. Scheduling and dispatching would have pace to it. Fleet maintenance and management would tap my mechanical skills and use up my excess energy. Rate regulations and inventory control are things I'd be interested in learning."

"All we need to have now," I said, " is evidence that you have the qualifications for such a job. That's what Part III of the Selectascope will tell us."

"All this jazz about a Selectascope. It's nothing more than gathering information and analyzing it."

"Of course," I agreed. "It's just a matter of selecting concrete questions and getting informed answers. Look, it's working, isn't it?"

"How am I going to convince an employer that I can handle scheduling and dispatching?"

"Follow the instructions in the questionnaire. Tell me about your background in terms of a job in a traffic department."

Even though on the surface Jim had nothing in his background directly related to traffic, we were able to piece together a combination of assets that made an attractive package. Remember, he did make his living in a transportation industry. He did know something about logistics and scheduling. He had a knack for repairing things—a handy skill to have around a fleet of trucks. We added other attributes to justify his candidacy. He had motivation and drive. Everything he'd done in the past pointed to his ability to get along with coworkers. More plusses.

We had to decide how to handle the fact that Jim knew nothing about rates and inventory. We would do the best we could—tell the truth. But instead of saying, "Sorry, I don't know anything about that," he would say, "That's one thing I want to know more about; I think I'd be good at it."

"There's something you ought to know," Jim said wryly. "I've been reading the classified ads for weeks and weeks. I've seen ads there for traffic managers, but I never thought of myself in that spot until you made me do my homework. The Selectascope really crystallized my ideas and put them all together."

Then Jim handed me an ad:

> ASS'T TRAFFIC MGR.: Loc. nat'l
> indust. firm needs asst. to traffic mgr.
> Exp. in fleet mgmt, scheduling, main-
> tenance, and rates. Call Mr. Nelson,
> 409-2120.

"Have you called?" I asked.

"Called—and got an appointment for tomorrow," Jim said proudly.

"What you've done this week has been the dress rehearsal for just such an interview." And I gave Jim one final but very important bit of advice. I recommended that he *not* give Mr. Nelson a résumé. Whenever your background on paper bears as little resemblance to the job requirements as Jim's did, *don't use a résumé*. Tell your story. Your own personal presentation will be far more persuasive.

Jim went to his interview full of confidence and optimism about his chances of being hired. The outcome proved him to be right; the Selectascope worked. Now Jim is working, too.

Effective action

Now is the time for every job seeker to put theory into practice. Effective action involves finding a prospective employer and arranging and preparing for an interview.

The interview is where it happens, where you realize that you're right for the job and the job is right for you. It is a time for you to get a fuller understanding of the job and the company, convince the employer that you're qualified for the position, project yourself, discuss goals and objectives, and negotiate salary. At the same time the employer judges your skills, intelligence, articulateness, and drive, and determines how well you perceive the job.

The following pages contain an edited version of the comments of a panel of experienced job seekers. Their successful job

53

campaigns earn them the right to be heard. You know them: Charles Wright, executive-on-the-ascent; Elizabeth Ziese, computer programmer, just hired; Jim Hobart, former pilot, newly employed; Mary Capra, office-manager-in-transition. I moderated the discussion:

BETH	It seems to me that job information is gotten the way people used to get sex information—from those who know the least. What's really the best way to find out where the jobs are?
CHARLES	For me, personal contacts have always been the best source, and then there's the *Wall Street Journal*, trade publications, and even daily business news.
MARY	I think you have to make a distinction between getting information about job openings for immediate use and gathering job ideas for long-range goals. Information about the latter is available in Dun and Bradstreet, directories of non-profit organizations, Chamber of Commerce literature, government publications, and even the Yellow Pages.
TAYLOR	Sometimes job information or job ideas can be turned into a job opening. I've known people who have created jobs for themselves because they sought out employers who generally needed their skills. Some employers were so impressed with their qualifications that they were offered specially created jobs even though the company had no plans to hire.
JIM	I thought that if you needed a job in a hurry you'd better use classified ads and employment agencies. But now I'd say you'd better take time to work out that Selectascope. Then at least you get a target in focus and you know what to look for.
BETH	If you use employment agencies, ask for recommendations from friends and personnel recruiters and pick those that specialize in placing people with your background. Try to find a counselor who takes a personal interest in you.

CHARLES	And if you're considering an executive search firm, remember, they're damned expensive and usually useless.
TAYLOR	Don't forget professional societies, college placement offices, and the United States Employment Service. No one has an exclusive in job leads. In addition, a job seeker can use one potential job as a prototype to generate others. After one employer has expressed serious interest, a person can approach other employers who have similar positions and do so with greater self-confidence.
CHARLES	Besides finding the right employer, the job has to be on the right level. I remember responding to one of those puzzling classified ads that leave too much to the imagination and discovering that the firm was looking for a man with twice my experience. You have to guard against that.
TAYLOR	I'll bet you know how now.
CHARLES	Right. Of course, salary range is one guide; so, sometimes, is the job title or the function of the person to whom you'll be reporting. That tips you off to the level of the job's responsibility.
MARY	What about when you're told repeatedly, "You're overqualified." It makes me furious. Is it just a way employers have of telling you that they don't want you?
TAYLOR	When the employer says "You're overqualified," he's referring to *his job,* not to *your skills.* Translated, he's saying, "The job is underqualified in terms of the skills you have to offer," meaning that your skills are not the ones for his job as he sees it. It's an attempt at being tactful, if not entirely truthful. Sometimes, of course, you may be interviewed for one particular position, but on the basis of a fuller understanding of your background be offered another.
BETH	Looking for a job is an education in itself.
TAYLOR	That's for sure! Well, what have you learned from it?
BETH	Be systematic. Keep records of whom you con-

JIM   tact, where you go, whom you see.
               Attitude is very important. You've got to be confident and optimistic, but also realistic.

CHARLES   Have definite goals. Employers respect candidates with concrete ideas about their career direction.

JIM   And don't pamper your pride. Spread the word that you're looking among friends, family, in-laws, second cousins—everybody.

BETH   If you plan to call companies to see if they have any openings, be sure you talk to the proper person and think out in advance what you want to tell him about yourself. Otherwise, the information you get or give is practically worthless.

MARY   I agree. I think it's preferable to send your résumé with a cover letter and follow up with a telephone call. Then at least you can have an intelligent conversation.

JIM   When I've called companies to arrange appointments for interviews for jobs I've seen advertised in the papers, I've literally had the interview on the phone and never even seen anyone in person.

TAYLOR   There's always a danger of saying too much on the telephone. You want to say just enough to create an interest in seeing you.

JIM   But suppose they keep asking you direct questions?

CHARLES   Be ambiguous. You know why Henry Kissinger is a diplomatic phenomenon? He's a master of creative ambiguity. You've got to be sharper than your competition.

TAYLOR   Another reminder—I think we tend to lose sight of how much competition there is out there. Just because you can't picture another candidate vying for the job you're trying to get, don't think he or she doesn't exist.

CHARLES   Mrs. Taylor, what's your thinking about bypassing personnel and middle management and

	going right to the top—contacting a V.P. or the president himself?
TAYLOR	Suppose I toss that question back to you. Since you've asked it, you probably have an opinion.
CHARLES	I'd say it depends on the job you're trying to get. If it's a top-level job, see the top man —unless you're angling for *his* job.
JIM	Do you ever look around at the people? I mean when you're on an interview, do you ever notice the employees? Their manner? Whether they seem to be interested in what they're doing?
BETH	Oh, I think you can definitely get a feeling of a company. Just the physical surroundings tell you what a company thinks of itself. You can almost feel whether you'd fit in.
MARY	Once I was on my way to an interview and it was in such a horrible building that I didn't even go in. I called to cancel the appointment—I forget the excuse I gave—but two months later that company moved to the newest skyscraper in town!
TAYLOR	That's a good lesson for everyone. Don't jump to conclusions.
JIM	I'm usually asked, "Where do you see yourself in five years?" I swear, I don't even know where I see myself in the next five days.
BETH	They always hit me with, "Why did you leave your last job?" In my case I had no problem with the questions—fuel shortages were not my fault—but suppose I didn't have a good reason?
TAYLOR	Ah! Now there's one of the toughest questions in the entire interview. Do you give a pat answer, such as "It's time to move along"? Do you give a real reason, such as "I didn't get the raise I was promised"? It's hard to generalize.
MARY	I think if you criticize your former employer, some of it rubs off on you.
TAYLOR	Good point! Don't dwell on the past. Use the question as a springboard to discuss your potential. Sometimes it's very difficult to give the

CHARLES   real reasons for leaving a job, or you may not even be able to verbalize them to yourself. The less said, the better. In any case, answer the question in a way which will be most advantageous to you. It's good to rethink the interviews you've had and get the answers to frequently asked questions firmly set in your mind.

MARY   I wonder whether personnel ever uses questions to trap you?

TAYLOR   I believe that questions should be weighed before they are answered regardless of who is asking or responding to them. Certainly the applicant who asks an in-depth question makes as favorable an impression as he would when he replies with an intelligent answer.

CHARLES   I often like to use questions to show my familiarity with a particular subject.

BETH   Your questions can even become a statement of your convictions.

JIM   Sometimes I've needed more time to think about my answer. When I've been stuck, I've asked, "Can you rephrase that question in more specific terms?"

BETH   I always try to frame my answers in the best possible light. For example, if I'm asked, "Have you worked with the RCA Spectra 70?" the correct answer is "No," but I would reply, "I've worked with the IBM 370, which is just about the same equipment."

MARY   You don't have to rush with your answers, either.

TAYLOR   That's a good point. First take a moment to ask yourself, "Why is he asking that question?"

CHARLES   If you really want to be sophisticated, listen for what is *not* being said. That in itself tells a story.

BETH   Listen, period. That's always good advice.

JIM   Funny, I listened to an employer go on and on for more than half an hour once, and do you know what he said to me at the end of the interview? "You express yourself very well."

TAYLOR   That was his way of telling you that you're a good
                listener, which always impresses an employer.

These people who have gone through the job search process
realize the difficulties involved. What they have learned along the
way will, hopefully, make your own search easier.

PART 3: HOW CAREERS FIND PEOPLE AND PEOPLE FIND CAREERS

Career equality for women

The occupational status of women is changing mostly because of women's changing views of themselves. Much of the progress in recruiting, hiring, and promotion of professional women is the result of women's own efforts to overcome discriminatory practices. Now that women are breaking out of stereotypical roles and are freer to act in ways that are consistent with their interests and values, there are both new opportunities and new responsibilities.

Emphasis in early life on vocational opportunities gives women a greater chance for career planning, education, and training. Today women are exploring ever-increasing career options and alternatives. Their new career choices reflect their new self-images.

In order to become the person you want to be, career planning must go hand in hand with life planning. Self-assessment, the first step, has already been discussed in depth. Completing your education and acquiring the necessary skills to pursue your objectives are of utmost importance. Don't stop short of gaining all the required credentials. Given your personal preferences and abilities, consider investigating fields in which as yet there are not many women employed. Learn what fields are expected to expand; you just may help insure your own economic future.

More women are gravitating towards nontraditional careers—engineering and law enforcement, even carpentry. If you keep your eyes open for innovative careers you may discover a field that meets your particular needs. And you may discover a new version of yourself.

Women are beginning to go where the men are to find career opportunities that offer higher earnings. It's getting easier and easier for women to enter occupations where men predominate. They can and should approach employers by pointing out the assets and aptitudes they have for their particular field. Who's going to teach employers that women have a valuable contribution to make? Somebody has to be first.

Once you have established yourself in your career it's important to take advantage of all possibilities for growth and professionalism. Even though there may be times when you are less active in your field, you can still keep up to date by furthering your education, affiliating with a representative professional society, or presenting papers at annual conventions.

You can advance your own career development by understanding employers' long-range goals and promoting your special abilities in terms of those goals. Are you a good communicator? A decision-maker? Do you bring new approaches to problem-solving or assume managerial responsibilities to demonstrate your professional effectiveness? These qualities can help you fulfill your own goals as well as those of your employer.

Women who are considering returning to the job market can learn much from those women who have already established themselves in careers. These following suggestions are based on their experiences. They may help you develop and implement your own objectives and goals.

First, are you ready to make a commitment to a career? Consider these internal and external factors: Are your attitudes, motivations, and energies focused on career planning? Are you at a stage of your life when these plans can be realized—either now or in the foreseeable future?

How do you start? Quiz yourself. What do you want a job to do for you? Your rationale for working is the foundation upon which you build your career plans. Do you seek a job because it will provide:

1. Professional growth
2. Income or additional income
3. The opportunity to make a useful contribution
4. Personal gratification

Before you can decide what you want to do, you must take a careful look at what you have done. Consider your:

1. Education
2. Extracurricular activities
3. Previous employment
4. Volunteer work
5. Hobbies
6. Interests

Next, paint a word picture of yourself. What are:

1. Your personality characteristics?

2. Your abilities and special skills?
3. The conditions under which you work best?
4. The things you enjoy doing?
5. The things you do best?

All this information will help you define your job needs. Now you must identify the kind of job that will satisfy those needs.

Jobs should be viewed from two aspects: the field and the function. For example, Urban Affairs is a field and research is a function. That is a broad generalization. Let's be more specific. A job in Urban Affairs in a non-profit organization is likely to be different from a job in Urban Affairs in private industry. One is profit-motivated; the other is not. A job in Urban Affairs might be concerned with housing, health, transportation, or education. A researcher working in any one of these narrower areas may be involved with statistics, data collection, analysis or evaluation. The work may require a math aptitude or writing capabilities. It might be done independently or in groups. Its purpose might be to provide background information for legislation or for public relations.

Once you have selected the field and function that interests you, reappraise your choice in these terms:

1. Do you have the educational requirements?
2. How much training is involved?
3. Will your innate skills and talents be further developed?
4. Will it provide the income you seek?
5. Is there potential growth?
6. Is the field itself expanding?
7. Will it give you the status you seek?
8. Does it serve your long-range goals?
9. Does it fit into your life style?

These questions may in turn raise other questions which need to be resolved. For example, should you further your education or seek a position which allows for on-the-job training? Should volunteer work be one of your alternatives? Volunteer work affords a pre-training opportunity that deserves your serious consideration.

Today volunteerism can be an apprenticeship to professionalism. It offers you the chance to determine the scope of your interest in a particular field and to test your aptitude for it. It introduces you to its members, who in time may assist your transition to gainful employment. It helps you learn to organize your work and family responsibility in such a way that both can be accomplished successfully.

Believe me, arriving at these decisions is far more complex than putting them into practice. Having done that, you are well on your way.

I believe that women, both individually and together, must exploit their political power if they are to gain equal rights in the true sense. In addition to equal pay for equal work, they must work for legislation that will guarantee equality in the Social Security system, pension plans, and insurance coverage.

Affirmative Action Programs to assure women's status at all levels of employment must be encouraged, supported, and implemented. To that end, women must take steps to monitor management's policies in order to remedy discriminatory practices and attain career equality. Commissions on the status of women are championing these causes; some unions are adding their voices; and all concerned individuals must give their spirited backing to accomplish this task.

Up the career ladder

Once a career is launched, most people set new objectives. They want to get ahead, find a better job with more money, increased responsibility, and greater security.

Men and women making their ascent up the career ladder will discover that career plans made now, five years ago, or five years hence have a number of things in common. One is the need to assess their current status. Another is the need to reappraise their goals.

It's introspection time again. Periodically you must take a reading of where you are and readjust your sights. The career with potential is always in motion, continually changing. (That even may be one of its attractions for you.) Meanwhile, you, too, are changing.

Let's say you were lucky enough to have chosen the right field. What about your particular job functions?

1. What are your likes and dislikes?
2. What part of the work do you do best?
3. What skills have you developed?
4. What other assets have you acquired?
5. What new knowledge have you gained?

Here is a concrete example of how to examine a career for the purpose of redefining its direction and capitalizing on individual strengths and interests.

Edward Mann was the reference librarian at Madison College. Had he wanted to, he could have remained there for all of his working days. His expertise was recognized, and he enjoyed an excellent reputation. Of course, he was eminently qualified for the position; not only did he hold a master's degree in library science, but his undergraduate degree was in international law—a discipline that was emphasized at Madison. After serving as a librarian for a while, Ed decided that he would like to apply his skills in a more challenging setting. He was eager to learn information retrieval techniques.

He accepted a position as a library technician with an educational consulting firm. Soon Ed realized that he had gone off on a tangent. The computer world was not his world, and he felt alienated by the mechanical aspects of the work. He knew he wanted to make a change, but he promised himself that he would not do anything until he fully analyzed his needs and preferences for the present and future and that then he would investigate job opportunities that he hoped would meet those needs.

Ed decided that job satisfaction was his first career priority. Furthermore, he defined his criteria for job satisfaction: working independently, in a research capacity, on an ongoing project in a field with which he could identify.

On the advice of a friend Ed considered a position as head librarian at an institute involved in drug abuse research. But the subject did not interest him. Ed explored opportunities in librarianship in the government, from the Library of Congress to the Naval Archives. He weighed the advantages and disadvantages. Advancement through the government ranks seemed to lead to heavy administrative responsibilities, and Ed was the first to admit that his strength did not lie in that direction. Even the security of such a position could not compensate for the disadvantages.

A professional librarian society recommended Ed for a position as bibliographer at the American Judicial Foundation. The foundation was funding a project to prepare a compendium of the decisions of Supreme Court justices. Now this really interested Ed, but as nearly perfect as the job seemed to be, he still had some nagging doubts. The most serious one was the fact that the position had a life of only three to five years. Then what? Should he risk having to go through this decision-making process all over again in about five years? His answer was a resounding yes. He reasoned: The job will give me the full measure of satisfaction I seek, and these new contacts might open the door to future possibilities in a law library—a thought Ed enjoyed contemplating.

Compare Ed Mann's approach to career development with Charles Wright's. Charles's concept of getting ahead was—and is—achievement-oriented, success-motivated, and measured in terms of power and prestige. He's with the company all the way, regardless of the company he's with. Advancement for Charles involves proving his competence and competing with his peers. He hardly ever questions himself about his career direction; he seems to sense it intuitively. He's more concerned about making it to the top. He thrives on responsibility, works well under pressure, and demonstrates qualities of leadership.

When Charles thinks of his future he concludes that what's good for the company is good for him. He's constantly expanding his knowledge of finance in particular and economic trends in general. He sees the interrelationship between his activities and the overall company objectives. He's a thinker, a planner, and a doer for his company—and himself. He will make it to the top, not just because of his outstanding capabilities, but also because he is willing to pay the price to get there.

On your way up the career ladder, you will make better choices and wiser decisions if you reappraise your progress from time to time.

Keeping your balance on the career ladder

"Am I in the right field?" Joseph Nesbitt asked me. "Why do I feel as if I'm going in circles?"

Sometimes you can discuss problems but you can't solve them. With effort, you can learn to cope with them. My counseling interview with Joe is a case in point.

Joe is the assistant credit manager of the Commercial Finance Corporation. Before that he was a claims adjuster for the AAA Insurance Company. And before that he was a management trainee at the Mercantile Bank.

According to Joe, his performance record on each job was outstanding. He described himself as an achiever with a talent for originating new systems and procedures. He had received many commendations for his work and several promotions along the way. Yet he never remained with one company for more than two years. Why?

Hear Joe tell it. "When I became supervisor at the bank I ran into some difficulties with the branch manager. I had some cost-saving ideas, but my boss wouldn't listen, so I took them to a vice president. Well, to make a long story short, I was thanked for the ideas, but they were never carried out, and after a couple of months, by mutual agreement, I left."

My mind started clicking. Was Joe so preoccupied with the need to prove himself that he was insensitive to the need to have good working relationships?

Then Joe explained what happened at the insurance company. "I really liked my work there. Everyone was business-minded. After just three months they were so impressed with me that they put me in charge of the department. I had fifteen employees under me and developed a plan to consolidate the clerical operation. In three weeks we were processing twenty percent more claims than previously. Can you imagine! I was able to reduce the staff and increase production at the same time."

Yes, I told myself, I could imagine that and lots more. I imagined that Joe really didn't understand how to motivate others. When he told me that the clerks in the department became "uncooperative," it confirmed my suspicion. He left the company, as I recall, because he felt he wasn't appreciated.

Joe was asked to leave his present position at the finance corporation. His tough-minded policies were affecting the company's goodwill image.

Now he's in my office. What am I supposed to tell him—that he doesn't know the first thing about getting along with people? I don't think you have to tell people what they probably really already know. I'm not going to change Joe, and I wouldn't try. Apparently in his mind only production and productivity count; the human element does not. So be it; I just have to take those facts into consideration when I make suggestions to him.

I told Joe that some people who are self-starters accomplish many objectives. If they care about results alone, then they should work alone. I recommended that if he wanted complete control, he ought to work in a situation where he has complete independence—where his responsibilities begin and end with himself.

Joe doesn't have to change fields or even change jobs frequently if he accepts one in which the functions of the job are limited to his individual activity.

Joe is learning to live with his problem and keep a job at the same time. He's working for the Williams Insurance Agency, running a one-man claims department. He's his own man.

Convertible careers

Every now and then a career takes an unexpected turn. Two such situations come to mind.

Phillip Robinson was an unusual civil servant. His achievements were neither unknown nor unsung. For twenty-three years, as a very able government employee, he had championed the causes of planned communities in the department now known as Housing and Urban Development.

Phillip was one of the architects of many of the codes, regulations, and land-use laws that are in effect today. His counsel and opinions were sought by state and local governments as well as private corporations and land developers.

A few years ago the firm of Deake and Fischer, real estate developers, approached Phillip with a proposal. They had acquired a half-million-acre tract of land in Arizona on which they planned to develop a self-sustaining municipality, and they wanted him to consider joining the firm as a senior vice president.

Phillip told me it was the kind of opportunity that he had never thought of before, but the thought intrigued him. He expressed his interest to Deake and Fischer, spent weeks poring over the plans—tax structures, transportation facilities, and resources—and then made a visit to the site. The idea of an urban area in a rural setting, with an industrial park, cultural center, and recreational facilities, captured his imagination.

Phillip had further talks with the officers of the firm, discussing financing and land use. He met with the board of directors to exchange views on planning and organizing the many facets of the project. There seemed to be general agreement concerning approach and objectives.

Phillip and his wife talked at length about the possibility of relocating to Arizona, and Phillip deliberated about the pros of the venture and the cons of his government job, the cons of the venture and the pros of his job. On balance he felt it was the kind of opportunity he couldn't afford to pass up.

Then he did a double take. "Wait a minute," he told himself. "How come I'm seriously thinking of leaving my job in the government? Whose idea was this in the first place? The thought would never have entered my mind! Is this really what I want?"

At this point he realized that he had allowed himself to be carried along on the crest of a proposition that, however fascinating, was not of his own making. "What do I need it for? I'm happy with what I'm doing," he told his wife. So with some lingering mixed emotions he wrote to Deake and Fischer expressing his decision to remain in the government. And the door was closed on that subject.

But a strange thing happened. Phillip found himself looking at his job from a new perspective. For some reason the work didn't satisfy him as much as it had in the past. After all, he had recently weighed its advantages and disadvantages and found it wanting. He took some leave time and went with his wife to their mountain cabin. He walked the trails, fished the streams, and contemplated his future. "This is the life, right here," he thought.

Now, on his own initiative, he began to think of alternatives to the career he had successfully built. Slowly the idea emerged—the time had come for him to put down on paper the mass of information he had acquired over nearly a quarter of a century. He decided to write a book. He resigned his job and wrote *The Principles of Urban Development in a Changing Society*. It was so well received that Phillip Robinson was invited to teach at Duquesne University, where he is now.

The other example of a "convertible career" concerns a woman whose first career was as a college professor—Helen Thomas, associate professor of home economics at Drexel Institute of Technology.

Professor Thomas was the institute's nutritional expert. More than that, she was a dedicated educator. Her students were keenly interested in her theories, and through the years she was asked for advice about dieting, health foods, and foods that prevented certain diseases. She counseled some students on their research projects and others on their laboratory techniques.

In 1972 two graduating students decided to open a health food store in West Philadelphia. Professor Thomas was very helpful to them, explaining that certain foods should be consumed for energy (sugar, starch, and fat), and others to supply nutrients to cells and tissues (amino acids, calcium, and vitamins). They stocked and carried a unique line of foods based on her recommendations. Then they added books and literature to their inventory. And once or twice Professor Thomas held open discussion meetings at the store.

Helen Thomas became so interested in the project that the following year she went into business with her former students. What would you call it? A case where the students influenced the professor? At any rate this was an instance of the career finding the person.

Switching careers

Switching careers is tough. It is tough because the world is so uncooperative. It wants dentists to keep filling teeth, accountants to add endless columns of numbers, and policemen to forever walk their beats. In this chaotic century people still like the orderliness of having other people typecast into roles even though they may have lost their original zest for their profession.

If you are to be successful in your threat to switch careers—and I use the word *threat* advisedly—you must be ready for a struggle. Not only will changing require all the inner resources you can call on—fortitude, drive, stamina, and self-confidence—but it may put a heavy burden on your financial resources as well.

So why do it? Do you really have the motivation? If you are certain that you do want to switch careers, take a backward look at where you've been before you take a step in a new direction. Question yourself about your present career:

Why did you choose it?
When did you choose it?

Did it accomplish what you hoped it would?
Are you well prepared for it both academically and
in experience?
How successful have you been?
What aspects of the work do you like? Dislike?
What aspects of the work do you do best? Least well?
What are your achievements?

Your answers are your road map. They are the signposts to
guide you to alternatives. Your objective is not to wipe the slate
clean and start anew, but rather to continue to use your previous
educational background, experience, and skills as fully as possible
and to adapt and transfer them from you present career to a future
career.

At no time is it more important to have a positive attitude
toward a job search than when you are switching careers. In a way
you are fortunate that you're able to give yourself a second chance.
But surprisingly, this is the one time not to think of turning yourself
into a "new" person!

A new career is the vehicle that allows the "old you" to develop
in a more satisfying environment. The more of the past you can take
with you the easier the transition will be.

Let's be practical. You want to switch careers either for external reasons such as inadequate income or for internal reasons involving personal gratification. The former reason is by far the easier
of the two to negotiate. In a sense, the decision is made for you by
circumstances beyond your control.

Keeping in mind your marketable skills, investigate fields related to your present career that avoid its problems to the greatest
extent possible. Surely this is neither original nor profound advice;
actually, you must do much the same things as everyone else who is
making a job search, only more so. Both the Selectascope you have
already read about and the Perceptual Résumé you will be reading
about in the next section are useful job guidance tools for you.

A career switch in search of some unfulfilled inner need is not
to be undertaken lightly. What good is it to divest yourself of six job-
oriented problems only to pick up a half dozen other problems?
Unless you really know what your inner needs are and that they are
likely to be satisfied, I consider switching careers very risky.

My advice is first to review what you do in terms of your field and your function. That is, perhaps you're in the right field but the wrong function, or vice versa. Take little steps before you take giant steps away from what you're doing now. Perhaps the problem is in more intangible areas—work-style or working conditions. If so, surely it can be mitigated without making drastic changes.

Of course, the ultimate decision is yours; if you are willing to take the risk, then make the move. And you might find the next discussion helpful.

Mini-careers

Some people, either by choice or circumstance, limit the scope of their involvement in an occupation. Mini-careers accommodate those job seekers who are especially interested in part-time or freelance work, consulting, or second careers. Some may have family responsibilities that preempt full-time career goals; others may have to limit their activities for health reasons; still others may be giving their prime efforts to endeavors that represent higher priorities for them. People also put limitations on their commitment to employment because they prefer flexible schedules or have circumscribed financial objectives.

Those who prefer mini-careers have one thing in common: they are likely to be in transition. Their careers are either winding down or starting up. These careers, then, are segments or abstracts of previous careers or prospective careers. Consider them in the context of larger career patterns, past or future. Here are a few practical suggestions.

Those who are considering switching careers might do well to explore their options through on-the-job training opportunities. Such semicareer positions can help job seekers decide whether their alternate choice is better than their original choice and whether additional educational preparation is necessary and worthwhile. For peace of mind alone, an experimental tryout has definite advantages. It's open-ended; you and your employer have limited expectations; and it can minimize mistakes that might be difficult to undo.

If a teacher is seeking another career, he might use the summer vacation to work with computers, or in a lab, or on a newspaper. None of these positions can be expected to be full-blown career opportunities. As temporary, low-level, easy-to-find jobs (because they are only steppingstones), they are foot-in-the-door chances to test interests and aptitudes.

A government employee considering a change, perhaps to consultant work for private industry, would be well advised to take a leave of absence to explore those possibilities before making a permanent decision.

Trial employment periods also provide no-strings-attached opportunities for military personnel preparing for their second careers. Both insurance companies and associations have been known to cooperate in this manner.

In all these instances the purpose of the mini-career is to keep your options open. In this way the job seeker does not put himself under undue pressure, get himself into untenable positions, or make premature decisions.

People who aspire to do free-lance research or writing are more or less on their own. Occasionally publishers will advertise in the classifieds for a free-lancer, but more often, free-lance jobs are obtained through personal contacts and recommendation, often by way of former full-time employers or fellow employees. Unknown free-lancers often must conduct a vigorous personal promotion campaign. In time, talent is discovered, recognized, and rewarded, and a kind of perpetual motion sets in.

Finding part-time employment can be difficult, but here's a suggestion. If you are looking for a short work week and a job that is a cut above clerical or routine work, keep it a secret! Search for a regular, full-time position *in the field for which you are qualified.* If your expertise is competitive in the open market and if an employer wants to hire you for a full-time position, he *may* hire you on a part-time basis. If the job is right for you and you're right for the job, make every effort to convince the employer of your outstanding qualifications. Avoid mentioning the subject of part-time employment as long as you can, hopefully until the job is offered. Then state your case the best you can.

Finally, there's one group for whom mini-careers are ideal—retirees. This is your chance, and you can afford to be very selective. Choose carefully, and pick out something fitting. Perhaps there's something you've always wanted to do?

If you're cautious by nature, it would be wise to select a job function you have enjoyed in the past and design your own position around it. For example, suppose you've been a fund raiser.

Anyone who has had a career as a fund raiser surely has developed excellent contacts. He also has had to do a great deal of detailed work. At this stage of your life, just pick the activity you prefer and enjoy it!

Some retired persons may feel that this is the moment they've been waiting for, and they may want to strike out on their own. Should you start your own business? Yes, of course—provided you know enough about the type of business you hope to establish. Naturally, if you've acquired a great deal of knowledge about the business you'd like to own as a result of years of experience in someone else's business (which is similar), that's ideal.

How many retired persons have a hankering to do something they've never done before? It's sort of like starting all over again. And that's exactly what it involves. It may require relearning or retraining. Just be sure you do plenty of planning.

PART 4: THE PAPER YOU

The résumé: what it does and doesn't do

More controversial advice is offered about résumé writing than any other aspect of job hunting. Do you state salary or not state salary? Use a photo or not? Keep it short or include all details? List references or not? In an era when the résumé has become a device for screening out or selecting candidates, you can ill afford to use a document that does not clearly convey your message to the reader.

Why all the difficulty? For one thing, you prepare résumés so seldom that it's not a practiced skill. For another, the subject is so subjective that you easily fall into rhetoric. And third, the objective of the résumé is often misunderstood.

Ideally, résumés wouldn't be needed; everyone would recognize and evaluate his or her qualifications precisely and know exactly when he could use them. And employers would judge each applicant in person. Often I have heard job seekers say, "If I can only get an interview. I know I can sell myself!" Instead, they are told all too frequently by personnel managers, "Send me your résumé." This is merely a dodge, a brush-off from employers who don't need what you have. When they do, they won't settle for a résumé as a stand-in for you, either.

But the market place is a vast arena, and the millions who work there cannot hope to know who needs whom to do what. And so the résumé has become the inevitable instrument to get your message across.

Though the résumé is a convenient way of eliminating inappropriate candidates, it also fails to provide vital information about appropriate applicants. Many things just can't be put on paper: how you organize your work, function under pressure, and get along with coworkers. The interview and only the interview allows this kind of information to be exchanged. That's where jobs are offered and accepted. The résumé, therefore, has a single function: *to get you an invitation to be interviewed.*

A good résumé may not land you a job, but a poor one may not even get you an interview. No interview, no job. It's as simple as that. A well-prepared résumé will initiate a series of favorable actions and reactions.

First, it will generate a sense of self-confidence that will be a boon to your job campaign. Directed to the proper market, it should trigger an immediate response. Then an initial interview in the personnel department promotes the possibility of your candidacy for employment, and at the same time gives you the chance to decide whether that particular opportunity is one you want to pursue. When you finally meet with the person you'll work for (and who has the hiring power), you can communicate your motivation, your drive, and your interest. You and your prospective employer can take each other's measure.

Above all, the résumé should present your qualifications in the best light possible and be as individual as your fingerprints. It should "tell it like it is"—your own individual background and experience—in your own way, your own words.

But before you dash to your typewriter to pound out your autobiography, set aside some think-time. Forget about dates, job titles, responsibilities, and references for a while, and take an overview.

The purpose of your résumé is to carry your message to a potential employer. If you were a plant manager at the Celanese Corporation and wanted to go to work for DuPont, you wouldn't need a résumé to tell your story. The similarity between the operations would make you an ideal candidate for such a position, and very likely you would have a contact at DuPont who would arrange an interview. The same situation applies when a stockbroker at Bache looks into possibilities at Merrill Lynch. Or when an assistant professor at Duke wants to move on, all she has to do is contact a few colleagues. So the résumé is your representative when you must reach out to spread the word of your availability beyond your circle of friends, contacts, and colleagues. Of course, they too will need a record of your credentials, but the basic résumé style adequately serves these situations. It is when your résumé is tossed out into the great unknown that you must state your case convincingly.

So first take a moment to consider who the reader of your résumé is likely to be. Your future may depend on whether he or she perceives the relationship between your qualifications and the requirements for the available position. Get a mental picture of this personnel person. There he is with this week's batch of résumés on his desk—316 to be exact—and with a trained eye he quickly sorts the bundle into three categories: yes, no, and maybe. The résumé that you will have spent hours preparing will be judged in two minutes!

First, résumés of persons whose backgrounds do not fall within the general parameters of the job requirements are eliminated.

The survivors are given more careful scrutiny. They are evaluated for similarity of experience, scope of experience, and educational preparation. Finally, from that group, a handful is selected. On paper their qualifications are closely matched with the requirements of the job to be filled. Their previous experience is likely to have been in organizations that provided related goods or services.

Believe it or not, over 90 percent of the résumés received will *not* be appropriate, whether the need is for an entry-level editorial assistant or for the controller of a multimillion-dollar corporation. One reason is an incomplete understanding of the job to be filled. The only time you can fully understand a job is when you've been doing it for a few years. That job is yours alone. Should someone else fill that same job, it will be different. The precise nature of a job changes with each job holder, and no job description can convey its details accurately, any more than even the best résumé can convey an accurate picture of a person. Words just cannot substitute for the dynamics of the job situation.

And this is a good explanation of why personnel managers themselves go through mumbo-jumbo rituals when they recruit. They just don't know all there is to know. But both job givers and job getters have a responsibility to interpret and state their cases as accurately as possible.

The second reason that most résumés miss their target is that they do not describe the job seeker's most marketable skills for a given job. Your chance for serious consideration increases significantly when your résumé is a factual account of your maximum achievement and you are as knowledgeable as possible about the company to which, and the position for which, you apply. Too many job seekers think that a résumé must be all things to all people, while just the opposite is true. The higher the level of the position sought, the greater the need for a specialized résumé.

Of course, you can't write a different résumé for each position, so you enclose a *cover letter* with your résumé. The letter is an opportunity to highlight in a more personal way those of your talents that a specific employer seeks. (Cover letters will be discussed in greater detail later.)

Another reason that résumés fail to elicit a response is that they include negative or limiting information that ought to be discussed in person rather than detailed on paper. Examples are previous salary or reasons for leaving other jobs.

Remember when you begin to write your résumé that it is a living document. The more you need to use it, the more you will need to revise it. When you send it off, tune in to the kind of waves it makes, for its mission is to get you in to see and be seen by a potential employer. Your message must be heard above the din created by your competitors.

The Perceptual Résumé

In order to write an effective résumé, you must perceive the relationship between your qualifications and the job market. It means understanding which of your capabilities are in demand and by whom. This insight is helpful whether you use the popular chronological résumé format or the familiar functional résumé format. It is imperative to use this approach when you are seeking a position that does not utilize your most marketable skills or when there is only an indirect or marginal relationship between your qualifications and the job's requirements. The result is a résumé style so different that I had to invent a new name for it: Perceptual Résumé. The Perceptual Résumé format emphasizes the similarities between skills offered and positions sought.

First, for job seekers with easily identifiable marketable skills—cartographers, demographers, oceanographers, and other specialists—who want employment in the field of their expertise, drafting a résumé is just a standard statement of education, experience, and accomplishments. If you are in this category, then go directly to basic résumé style (see the next section).

For others, let's look at the facts. What have you done with yourself so far? Are you fluent in Spanish, Italian, Arabic, and Hindustani? Do you want a job that requires using those skills? If the answer is yes, then those talents become your most marketable skills and claim the limelight on your résumé. These language qualifications are what you are advertising and promoting.

Once you know what you want an employer to know about you, you have identified the very essence of your résumé. From it flows the form and pattern your résumé will take. The task is laid out for you, and the steps follow easily; you show that you *can* do what you *want* to do.

However, many job seekers don't *want* to do what they can do. They may be looking for a position that does not utilize their marketable skills; they may want to enter a field in which they have secondary abilities rather than primary ones. This, of course, poses both a complication and a challenge: to design a résumé that *appears* to show the capability for a particular position. The Perceptual Résumé solves that problem.

Briefly, to create a Perceptual Résumé, you begin by writing a job description of the kind of position you are seeking. Then you prepare a biographical outline including education, experience, and all accomplishments. Next, the trick is to perceive what both have in common. Find the similarities between the position and your skills. Of course, the more closely they are related, the more convincing a case you can make to a prospective employer.

Here is an example of the development of a Perceptual Résumé. Jon Tasha taught Spanish and geography at Clarendon Community College for three years. He decided that teaching had become too remote and passive for him. He wanted a position in which he would play a more active and productive role. Meanwhile, the energy crisis had reordered national priorities and created a growing need for people with experience in, and understanding of, the economic and technical aspects of our natural resources. Even though his training and experience were primarily in the field of foreign language, he believed he also had enough background in geography to justify his candidacy for a position involving the supply and utilization of energy.

Jon wrote a job description, a prototype of the position he wanted to get:

> Assist with planning and development of projects related to the supply/utilization/distribution of fuel (oil, gas, coal) and requiring the ability to gather and evaluate data.

Then he prepared a biographical outline:

> M.A., Spanish Language and Literature
> B.A., Geography
> Assistant Professor, Spanish Grammar and Composition (two years)
> Instructor, Geography Department (one year)
> Summer Employment: scheduling interchange of rail traffic; calculating rates.
> Hobby: Geology

Jon then had to develop a strong case, presenting evidence that his background deserved serious consideration by a company engaged in producing, mining, refining, or transporting fuel products. He emphasized his knowledge of geography, geology, and transportation. At the same time he deftly de-emphasized other qualifications without tampering with the truth.

Here is Jon's Perceptual Résumé:

RÉSUMÉ

Jon Tasha	Single	Age: 26

Address: 3313 Brewster Road #631
         Riverdale, Kentucky 20840
Phone: (620) 927-7991

EXPERIENCE:
SPECIALIST IN ECONOMIC GEOGRAPHY
Clarendon Community College, Clarendon, Kentucky, 1972 to present
- Reported on the industrial, mining, and agricultural characteristics of the U.S.
- Surveyed trade routes and transportation facilities
- Prepared studies related to the distribution of raw materials
- Organized field trips to shale oil tracts
- Investigated strip mines
- Developed projects related to erosion
- Prepared charts and maps
- Taught Spanish

DISPATCHER AND RATER
Southern Railways, Atlanta, Georgia, 1968-1972 (part-time)
- Scheduled freight traffic
- Coordinated connecting trains and interchanges
- Calculated shipping costs
- Recorded statistical data concerned with shipments, volume, and revenue

EDUCATION:
B.A. Economic Geography 1971
Dickinson College, Carlisle, Pennsylvania
Honors and awards: Full four-year scholarship; National Geographic Society Award for excellence in Physiography
M.A. Spanish 1972
Indiana University, Bloomington, Indiana

HOBBY:
Geology: Investigating and studying the age of rocks

This Perceptual Résumé generated three interviews and two job offers, and Jon went to work for an oil company that leased federal tracts for shale mining. His position was in the department responsible for minimizing the adverse environmental effects of the shale processing plants. This involved complying with government regulations for the disposition of used shale and controlling toxic by-products and pollutants.

Jon had done a masterful job of bringing into focus specific information while not drawing attention to other facts. The first decision he made was to place his *experience* first. The rationale was that he would be able immediately to indicate some substantive knowledge of problems related to natural resources. Then he invented a job title for himself, one that he believed would elicit a positive reaction from those he was trying to reach. Putting "Specialist in Economic Geography" *above* "Clarendon Community College" set the tone of the résumé and gave a more favorable impression. Wisely, he neither referred to teaching (except Spanish) nor used academic terminology. Words like *reported, surveyed, studies,* and *investigated* suggested a research activity. And this was, in fact, part of his work. Note that he hedged somewhat by calling his summer employment "part-time." He hoped that the vagueness would conjure up a longer period of employment than was actually the case.

Jon handled the *education* bloc in an unorthodox fashion, but it served his purpose. Had he used the traditional approach, his M.A. in Spanish, which added little to his dossier, would have been listed ahead of his B.A. in Economic Geography, which carried more weight. (Properly, the statement about your education begins with the highest academic degree achieved, unless you're a Ph.D. candidate, in which case I'd allow an exception. But *never* begin this bloc by naming your junior high school!)

Whether your Perceptual Résumé begins with an account of your academic background or your experience depends on which is more convincing proof of your capability for the job you are seeking. A hobby, which Jon listed, should be included only if it is pertinent.

Basic résumé style

Now that you've been introduced to the Perceptual Résumé, take a look at the basic résumé style.

RÉSUMÉ

Alice McGowan
14 Edgehill Drive
Chicago, Illinois 66641
(326) 797-1478 (home)
(326) 832-4192 (office)

Job Goal:	Personnel, with emphasis on recruitment and selection of staff; Administration
Education:	B.A. Psychology, Purdue University
1956	Lafayette, Indiana
Employ-	Personnel Manager
ment:	NATIONAL SAFETY ASSOCIATION
1959-	Chicago, Illinois
present	Responsible for all professional, secretarial, and clerical recruitment and selection for staff of 950 employees. This involves working with college and university placement offices, public and government agencies concerned with minority placement, state and local safety associations, and public and private employment agencies, and placement of advertisements in Chicago and out-of-town newspapers. Complete understanding of total personnel parameters: job classification, benefits package, and wage and salary program. Chairman of NSA Inservice Education Committee. Developed staff training programs. Conducted orientation workshops. Provided career advancement counseling to employees. Supervisory responsibility.
1956-	Administrative Assistant to Director
1958	AMERICAN SCIENCE ASSOCIATION
	Akron, Ohio
	Duties included attending executive committee meetings, preparing agenda items, taking minutes, and writing summary drafts; served as advertising manager of the Association's journal; interviewed applicants for clerical positions and supervised office staff; handled all requests to purchase member-

	ship lists of the Association as well as serving as personal secretary to Dr. Ernest Shoemaker.
Professional Member- ships:	Member, National Personnel Association Secretary-Treasurer, National Management Association, 1967-1971
Personal Data:	Date of Birth: February 7, 1935 Marital Status: Married, 2 children
References:	Available upon request

This format can be modified in an almost infinite number of ways. Your presentation will depend on the image you want to convey, the credentials you want to emphasize, and the material you want to highlight. Every bloc—education, experience, and personal data—should be arranged in a way to capture and hold the eye of the reader so that you will be invited for an interview.

Test your résumé by imagining that you were charged with hiring someone with your background. Does the résumé get its message across clearly and briefly? Does it accentuate your strong points and minimize your limitations? And again, does it couch your experience in terms of the employer's interest? Have you used active, descriptive language to convey your responsibilities and duties? (For example, "supervised staff" is an improvement over "two clerks assisted me.")

In the basic résumé style, "Job Goal" can be replaced with "Objective" or "Summary of Experience," but I recommend that this bloc be used only when you have something specific to say and when it can be said in twenty-five words or less. "Economic research and analysis" is fine. But "I am interested in a position in which I can utilize my leadership ability and communicative skills to motivate people and organize data for analysis and implementation" is *not* fine.

You can be innovative in the organization of your information. For example, the treasurer of a bank may feel it is more advantageous to identify his position before he names the bank:

Treasurer
Denver City Bank

However, if the firm is prestigious, one might promote his fortunes this way:

> Chase Manhattan Bank
> Treasurer

The inclusion of your age on your résumé depends on whether you consider it an advantage or not. Its omission always raises questions, and, whether you are young or mature, you may be more self-conscious of your birth date than the reader is. Everyone has an age. You decide whether indicating it adds to your qualifications or not.

Creating a word picture of yourself

Over the years I've collected a file called "Things *Not* to Do on a Résumé." Whenever I read a résumé that seems to defeat its purpose, a copy of it goes into that file. I've selected some examples for you to review, hoping they will help you avoid making the same errors.

To put more than necessary in a résumé only invites confusion, distracts the reader, detracts from what you have to say, and raises questions that might eliminate rather than reinforce your candidacy.

Study this résumé carefully. A critique will follow.

VIRGINIA DUNN

Home Address
47 Macomb Rd.
Apt. 17
Dayton, Ohio 43202
(210) 263-9730
PERSONAL DATA:
Age: 23
Marital Status: Single
Birth Date: June 14, 1949
Available:
Immediately

Address as of
January 15, 1973
3619 N. 24th Street
Fairfax, Virginia 22265
(730) 237-3769

Health: Excellent
Height: 5' 4"
Weight: 127
PROFESSIONAL OBJECTIVE:
A responsible permanent position in a public relations or personnel capacity where experience and creativity may be fully utilized.
EDUCATION:

Degree:	Graduate, 1967, of Madison High School, 7077 Park Rd., Dayton, Ohio.
Major Subjects:	(College Prep)
	English Literature (A average)
	French (A average)
	Business Law and Consumer Economics (A average)
	Principles of Democracy (A average)
	Sciences: Biology, Chemistry (B average)
Extra–curricular:	Student Council Representative
	Y-Teens, Inter-Club Council Representative
	Girls Athletic Association
	Senior Class Committee
	Senior Class Play
College:	1967-1972, Ohio State University, College of Arts and Sciences
Major:	Journalism, Newspaper Editorial and Public Relations Emphasis
Major Courses:	Reporting and editing sequences, communications law, photojournalism, public relations principles and practices
	(Major cumulative grade-point average, 3.1)
Other Courses:	English, Spanish, History, Political Science, Philosophy
Extra–curricular:	*Ohio State Lantern* Staff
	(College Newspaper)
	Editorial Assistant *Literary Review*
	Active Member and Secretary, Kappa Tau Alpha (National Journalism Scholastic Society)
EXPERIENCE:	

March–December, 1972	Worked with the Director of Corporate Communications at Cosmos Companies, a Dayton, Ohio-based, regional real estate development firm. Various responsibilities included dealing with the public on matters of general media interest, distributing news releases to local and national publications, and general office activities including typing, Dictaphone, and receptionist duties.
Reason for Leaving:	To seek a more challenging and diversified position.
February–August, 1971:	National Planning, Inc. Worked as a typist with promotion to Shift Supervisor. Had responsibility for approximately 20 production MTST typists. Responsibilities also included hiring, interviewing, scheduling, production, and conduct of employees under my direction.
Reason for Leaving:	Returned to Ohio State University to continue studies.
Summer 1968-69:	Kelly Services, Inc. Was employed in a variety of executive secretarial and receptionist positions requiring diversified business skills (e.g. typing, Dictaphone, Addressograph, adding machine, and switchboard) and the ability to deal with the public.
Reason for Leaving:	To continue classes at Ohio State University.
OFFICE SKILLS:	Type approximately 55-60 wpm (am familiar with IBM Selectric, Executive, and Standard typewriters). Have operated various Dictaphone machines extensively and have no difficulty in adapting to different models. Have used both manual and automatic Addressograph machines for the purposes of distributing data on a mass information basis. Also have experience with various adding

89

machines, Xerox equipment, and switch-board operation.

LOGICAL EVAL-UATION: Through experience, education, travel, and general initiative, have developed the ability to determine the merits of a given proposal by quickly separating facts from conjecture in areas where competition and results achieved were the criteria of success.

Virginia Dunn's résumé demonstrates many common errors. First, if you use a "home" or "permanent" address with a "temporary" or "current" address, it is the first clue to the reader that you are not settled in the community. This impression can jeopardize your consideration at the very start. Whenever you can, use just one address. You may, however, list two telephone numbers, one for home and one for office or "for messages."

In the Personal Data bloc, listing both age and birth date is redundant. Height and weight (along with color of hair and eyes) belong on your driver's license, not on your résumé. Such details only detain the reader from getting to your important message—what you can do for him.

Concerning the use of "Professional Objective" there are two schools of thought. Those who recommend its use claim that a succinct statement about your capability quickly identifies you; and there are those who feel that such a statement is too restrictive. My own advice is to leave the decision of where you fit in to the one who receives your résumé. Don't create limitations for yourself. If your record proves what you can do, it doesn't need a prefacing statement; the facts speak for themselves.

In addition, a résumé that is circulated at large is not the place to tell what you would *like* to do. Save that for the interview. If the employer discovers that you *can* do what he wants done, that's when you bargain for assurances that your career objectives will be met.

Virginia Dunn put two objectives—not even remotely related—in her résumé. At the very least, this confuses the issue and dissipates the emphasis on her best qualifications. In this case it also reveals a total lack of understanding of the qualifications required for positions in PR and personnel.

In describing her education, Virginia sets the wrong tone by starting with her high school graduation (quite a comedown from her lofty professional objective). Next, she makes the error of listing her major subjects and compounds it by including grades. Not very apropos. While Virginia is using valuable space to provide extraneous information, she is losing her reader.

My complaint about the college information is that the material is poorly organized. The major should stand out when you want to trade on it. This is easily achieved if you don't clutter up the bloc with a list of courses. Subjects within a major need not be listed; if you include them, it is assumed that you have little else to say. I would also expect a journalism major to report all data. That means indicating the location of Ohio State University (Columbus, Ohio), a standard practice when location is not generally known.

In the experience bloc Virginia has mistakenly emphasized some information that does not convey a favorable impression. Staying for nine months on one job and six on another is nothing to be exactly proud of, and this information should not be in such a prominent spot. Dates should be taken out of the margin and buried somewhere within the copy.

As I've said before, I almost always object to including reasons for leaving on a résumé. Virginia's "to seek a more challenging and diversified position" is going to raise the question in the reader's mind, "Will Miss Dunn consider the job in my company challenging or even diversified?" The important question is "Can Virginia Dunn do the job?" Don't be so eager to tell too much. The only possible reason for including "reason for leaving" is to promote your cause or create a positive impression. One such example might be "relocation." But then to be consistent you'd have to give your reason for leaving every job, and this can be very awkward. Even "merger" or "reorganization" has a negative tinge—why didn't you fit into the merger or reorganization? Wait until the interview, when something like that can easily be explained.

The office skills section of Virginia Dunn's résumé is, of course, the dead giveaway. *This* is what Virginia Dunn can really do, as the details in this bloc very specifically tell the reader. Virginia's familiarity with various types of office equipment proves to the employer that she is qualified—*for a secretarial position.* Is that what Virginia wants? Not according to her professional objective. Rather than convincing the employer that she is a professional, Virginia has only proved that she is a nonprofessional applicant.

These comments are primarily suggestions for revision of the form and format of Virginia's résumé. But more serious than errors in format is Virginia's failure to understand the *level* of the position she might logically be considered for. Even her own "logical evaluation" is touching without saying anything substantive.

Logically Virginia might expect to be considered for an entry-level position in journalism if her strength is in writing and reporting or as an editorial assistant if her competence and interest lie in that direction. More positions of the latter kind exist, but if she prefers the former, she can make her case by strongly emphasizing writing/reporting talents while only indirectly indicating editorial skills.

Here is Virginia Dunn's revised résumé:

VIRGINIA DUNN
3619 N. 24th Street, Fairfax, Virginia 22265
(730) 237-3769

<u>Education</u>
B.A. in Journalism 1972
Ohio State University, Columbus, Ohio
Extracurricular activities:
Staff Reporter, *Ohio State Lantern*
Editorial Assistant, *Literary Review*
Member, Kappa Tau Alpha (National Journalism Scholastic Society)

<u>Experience</u>
Communications Assistant 1972
Cosmos Companies, Dayton, Ohio
Distributed news releases to local and national publications. Responded to inquiries concerning corporate activities. General office duties.
Supervisor 1971
National Planning, Inc., Dayton, Ohio
Responsible for the work flow of 20 typists. Scheduled production of manuscripts. Proofread copy. Checked copy for grammar and spelling.
Summer Employee 1968-1969
Kelly Services, Inc., Dayton, Ohio

Various secretarial and receptionist positions requiring diversified business skills and the ability to deal with the public.

Personal Data

Birth Date: June 14, 1949; single

Samples of published news and feature stories available upon request.

This revised résumé will leave no doubt in the reader's mind that Virginia has the basic requirements for a job in the word business. And without having to state it, Virginia is telling the reader she is looking for an entry-level position. This résumé should not be placed in contention for anything else. Suppose Virginia learns about the need for an editorial assistant on the staff of an economic or medical journal. Having been told that they may be interested in a beginner, she should then stress her familiarity with consumer economics or the sciences in her cover letter without, however, being too specific about the extent of that familiarity or when she acquired it.

Determining the level of responsibility for any given position is a very delicate problem indeed. Often it's difficult for job seekers to tell whether a position is senior, junior, or mid-level. So once you have evaluated your own level of experience, examine the flip side of the problem. The more you can learn about the job, the more accurately you can gauge the qualifications being sought. Salary, participation in policy-making, range of expertise, and scope of supervisory duties give some indication of the level of responsibility of a position. These are the facts you must gather. Unfortunately, they are elusive and very difficult to pin down.

Employers manage to complicate the problem when the position is not clearly defined in their minds. For example, to recruit for a position "in the fifteen- to twenty-five-thousand dollar range" or with "salary open" or "salary commensurate with experience" only invites misunderstanding.

Sometimes employers launch a search for a candidate just to survey the field and discover who's available at what price. Management may want to know current salary trends or the mix of experience it might find for certain positions. You can keep your own mistakes to a minimum if you are sensitive to the implications of job information. There is much to be learned from what is *not* said about a position. The following ad in the classified pages of a local newspaper is a case in point.

FINANCIAL COPYWRITER: We need a creative, hard-hitting writer, experienced in financial businesses for our in-house ad agency. This is an opportunity to grow with an aggressive, rapidly expanding regional financial services organization. The right person should have an all-around background in print, radio, TV, and brochures. Salary commensurate with experience, excellent company-paid benefits, and convenient suburban location.

Please submit résumé along with salary history: FIRST CORPORATION, Employment Office, 6400 Boulder Rd., Falls City, Pa.

Equal Opportunity Employer

This is a deceptive ad. The employer has no serious interest in writing ability. That's just a come-on. The tone of this ad is money, money, money. And only those interested in getting, saving, or spending it need apply. The use of the phrase "our in-house ad agency" is dubious and misleading. Words like "hard-hitting" and "aggressive" have a distinct sales-pitch approach; "all-around background in print, radio, TV, and brochures" is almost an impossibility, and the words are merely a lure because they are glamor words. My guess is that this is a commission sales job. People with experience or an interest in radio or TV will be duped if they respond. The lack of detail about the "all-around background" is almost an open admission that the words are used to entice rather than to explain the position.

Were you to explain your background in the language of the foregoing ad, it too would have the empty ring of vagueness with intent to create a false impression.

The following advertisement, on the other hand, is complete in its description of the position to be filled.

TECHNOLOGY EXCHANGE: A Washington, D.C.-based public service company has an immediate opening for a top-flight Director of Information Systems ($18,000-$20,000). Computer systems experience requirements include IBM 370, IBM 360, Univac 1108. Language proficiency requirements include FORTRAN and COBOL. Sound working knowledge required in areas related to library and information services with data base systems. Creative ability required for systems conceptualization, analysis, and design. Superior writing and editing skills required. Please forward résumé, salary history, and hardware experience summary to: TECHNOLOGY, INC., 1 Charles Circle, Washington, D.C.

Here the level of responsibility is clearly spelled out in the function of the job—"systems conceptualization, analysis, and design" are the key words. Regardless of hardware experience or writing ability, only those who meet the requirements for the level of responsibility need apply. The implication is that there will be responsibility for supervising and directing the work of others. This ad talks to those trained in the field and is Greek to others.

Technology, Inc., received seventy-eight résumés and interviewed two candidates. Andrew Laslett was one of them. Here is his résumé.

ANDREW LASLETT

446 21st Street
Washington, D.C. 26036
(220) 244-7289

EXPERIENCE
July 1972 to Present
Washington Operations, General Energy Company

95

<u>Director, Information Services</u>
Provide policy guidance and direct activities of Technical Information Services and Library Services, with 45 personnel including three other supervisors. Functions include writing, editing, and responsibility for technical library center and automated information retrieval systems (COBOL).
July 1969 to July 1972
American Communications Corporation
<u>Supervisor, Publications and Reproduction</u>
Organized Publications group, establishing systems, procedures, and standards and training personnel. The group produced all company documentation including public relations releases. Writing, editing, copy preparation, and graphic arts functions were centralized. Responsible for all reproduction and photographic services. Offset printing capability was self-contained. Photographic services included motion pictures.
August 1966 to June 1969
Technidyne Corporation
<u>Senior Programmer</u>
Responsible for testing and evaluating library programs for the Space Flight Center library maintenance contract. Duties consisted of analyzing and correcting problems encountered within programs in the library and determining the suitability of new programs for inclusion within the library structure. These library programs included orbit determination, equipment status, astrophysical-geophysical data analysis. The project consisted of 760 FORTRAN programs.
EDUCATION
M.S. Computer Sciences 1966
Clarkson College of Technology
Potsdam, New York
B.A. Logic and Philosophy 1965
Beloit College, Beloit, Wisconsin
PROFESSIONAL MEMBERSHIPS
Society for Technical Communication, Senior Member
American Management Association
PUBLICATIONS
"Basic Systems and Procedures," *AMA Digest,* New York City, November 1972

"Improving Technical Communication," *Technical Communication,* pp. 12-16, Fourth Quarter 1971

Résumé writing: more don'ts and do's

Although most companies have forms that ask for much of the same information that goes in a résumé, never send out a replica of a company form in lieu of your résumé. It makes very dull reading, and its function differs from that of a résumé. The résumé is your tool to tell your story; the employer's application is his tool to gather information, including data and vital statistics that do not belong on a résumé. Examples are your Social Security number, starting and final salary, and reasons for leaving.

Likewise, do not use an outline lifted from the government's Form 171. The format and content of the information do not serve your needs. It's an official document for official use.

Never use a company job description as an account of your duties and responsibilities, but always write a statement about your position in your own words. Only you can project the full flavor of what you did. Company job descriptions read like a manual of instructions and make every job seem as if it was performed by a machine.

In your own résumé it is possible to be original. Here is a worksheet—a list of job likes and dislikes—that Charles Davis prepared *for his own personal use.* This is the kind of self-examination I recommend for both planning a new job and writing a résumé.

Job Likes and Dislikes

A. What I want from a job
1. Recognition
2. Variety of duties
3. Contact with people
4. Some out-of-office work
5. Writing/interviews
6. Responsibility and freedom
7. Relaxed environ-ment (informal)
8. Tangible proof of accomplishment
9. Pride in organization/product
10. Chance to motivate people
11. Chance to learn something—self-educating

B. <u>What I don't want</u>

1. Too much pressure	5. An all-writing job
2. Work at home	6. Company politics
3. Travel away from D.C. area	7. Paperwork
4. Just a few people in office(?)	8. Too many duties to do each effectively

C. <u>Goals, future</u>
1. See myself as a proven creative and responsible communicator—oral, written.
2. Functional—I can communicate in a wide variety of organizations.
3. Oral communicator
   a. Motivate people, supervise
   b. Work together with people
4. Written communicator
   a. Newspapers
   b. Letters, memos

The product of this preparation is a well-organized résumé that gets its message across effectively.

CHARLES DAVIS   4316 Taylor Lane
Chevy Chase, Md. 20910
(361) 689-9416

<u>OBJECTIVE</u>: Creative and responsible position as editor, advertising manager, or public relations administrator.

<u>SUMMARY OF QUALIFICATIONS</u>: Proven record of responsible managerial experience, coupled with documented creative work in public relations, advertising, and journalism. Prime assets include ability to communicate ideas and motivate people.

<u>WORK EXPERIENCE</u>:

<u>Advertising and Publicity Manager</u> . . . of a data processing firm . . . responsible for directing and implementing entire publicity program . . . designed and contracted for advertisements . . . prepared all news releases . . . wrote feature articles that appeared in leading computer journals . . . pro-

vided salesmen with more creative sales materials . . . worked closely with local advertising agency in extensive market research . . . designed brochures . . . responsible for exhibits at national trade shows . . . initiated direct mail campaign . . . prepared and implemented advertising budget . . . engaged in layout and production work.

What the Vice President said: "Communicates well with sales . . . excellent success in approaching journal editors ... well received at all levels from office staff to corporate management . . . enthusiasm is contagious . . . does a quality job."

Writer, Editor, Columnist . . . over 3 years journalistic experience . . . won First Place in Maryland-Delaware Press Association Contest for Newswriting . . . wrote feature articles, editorials . . . as sports editor, responsible for producing and supervising the sports section . . . experience in layout, copy editing, and production.

What the Editor said: "I consider this young man a talented writer . . . . He is thoughtful and responsible and should be considered for a position that offers him a chance to use his initiative and innate enthusiasm."

Administrator . . . as Administration Manager for a major computer corporation . . . responsible for all the administrative, accounting, personnel, and customer relations activities of the Washington branch office . . . supervised the entire clerical staff . . . worked directly with the salesmen to assist their marketing effort . . . aided the branch manager in his communications with upper management . . . worked directly with upper management on pilot work study program.

What the Branch Manager said: "Mr. Davis did an outstanding job for us in all areas. One of his particular strengths is his ability to motivate people . . . he is completely marketing oriented . . . he has one of the most positive attitudes of anyone I have met within NUSIVA."

EMPLOYMENT DATES

As an Advertising and Publicity Manager at the Fenwick Corporation (1969-present)

As a Writer, Editor, and Columnist at the William County *Sentinel* and the Maryland *News* (1966-1969)

As an Administration Manager at NUSIVA Division of Falcon, Inc. (1964-1966)

EDUCATION

Williams College (B.A. degree 1964), Williamstown, Massachusetts; Executive Council; Theta Delta Chi fraternity; Writer, College Yearbook; Varsity Soccer Captain; B average Governor Academy, Newton, Massachusetts (graduated 1960) Senior Class President; Yearbook Editor; Baseball and Basketball Captain; Honor Roll.

PERSONAL DATA

31 years of age, married (no children)

References and reference letters will be furnished upon request.

This is the kind of résumé that makes the person charged with hiring say, "I'd like to meet the author of this résumé." Clear thinking and good organization are requirements for many jobs and the person who shows these qualities—even on a résumé—will surely be sought. Charles Davis's résumé had always been effective in the past, and now that Davis has decided not to follow his company to its new location, his résumé is opening new doors to job opportunities.

The next résumé gets off to the wrong start by providing too much personal data and by placing "Hobbies and Interests" so prominently, telling the employer what's uppermost in the applicant's mind. Stick to the old Puritan ethic—work before play.

Name: John Thomas
Social Security No.:
129-68-4915
Birth Date: April 19, 1945
Birth Place: Ithaca, N.Y.
Height: 5' 10"
Weight: 165 lbs.
Health: Excellent

Address: 34 Adams Street
Clipton, Md. 21401
Phone: Home (361) 861-3946
Office (202) 229-4071
Marital Status: Married to
Margaret Ann
Dependents: One
Military: Draft status is I-Y

Hobbies and Interests: travel, sailing, skiing, camping, tennis, photography, music, current history, and politics.

Professional Skills: managerial ability, good public speaker, ability with all forms of writing (e.g. ad copy, news copy, editing, script, pamphlet, report, research, letter, speech, creative), film and audio-visual production, layout, still photography, typing (60 wpm).

Needless to say, résumés should be immaculately typed and every word spelled correctly. In addition, I consider it more professional to use complete words than abbreviations—that is, *New York* not *N.Y.* I object to the use of *3/70* instead of *March 1970.* Never include the day *(March 15, 1970).* And whenever possible, eliminate the month as well. Doesn't it look more substantial to write 1970-1971 than 3/70-8/71?

Do not refer to *Health* unless it is excellent. If you are not married at the time you write your résumé, then you are single (not divorced, separated, widowed). Never indicate race, creed, or nationality on your résumé. *It's illegal.* Sending your photograph is risky. (Beauty is in the eyes of the beholder.) Watch your clauses: "Married, with three children, in excellent health." Who is in excellent health—you or they? Do not reveal nonpertinent information gratuitously. Look at this excerpt.

Objective: Association with a company which appreciates and utilizes that type of metallurgical knowledge gained only by experience and maturity.

Doesn't this engineer sound a little self-conscious about his age?

I personally object to résumés written in the first person, but I object doubly when they are poorly organized.

A product of the Columbus, Ohio, school system, I entered Purdue originally to study engineering. After two years in engineering, I changed majors to political science and journalism because of my fascination with newspaper work. I speak one foreign language—French. A district Golf Association caddy scholarship paid part of my tuition all four years at Purdue.

Work experience: I worked three and one-half years for the *Western Exponent* and one year as a stringer for *The New York Times.* While with the *Exponent* I was editor-in-chief for my senior year, copy editor for a year, and a desk editor for six weeks. In addition, I have worked in offset composition, in the offset darkroom, and in the pressroom on a three-unit Goss Community press. I am a fairly accomplished photographer, owning my own Nikon equipment.

My work for *The Times* was done during my senior year and included feature articles and some spot news. In high school I worked at the Lake Country Club as a caddy. During college I worked for two summers on the grounds crew at the Lake Country Club.

And keep it short. Think of the poor reader, and if you can't, then think of yourself. The following résumé will find its way to the round file fast. It won't be read because the format is dull and unimaginative.

Since graduation from the University of North Dakota in June, 1970, I have been employed as Field Secretary and Chapter Consultant for the national executive offices of my college fraternity, Pi Tau Phi, which position I resigned this June. My chief duty was to travel around the country to the local chapters of the fraternity, acting as liaison and trouble-shooter for the national. On the road I did such things as straightening out financial problems, mediating disputes, obtaining housing and services at minimal cost, raising funds, showing declining organizations how to attract and keep members, consulting and negotiating with college officials, recruiting, speaking publicly, and teaching undergraduates in all phases of chapter operations. The late nineteen sixties was a crucial time for fraternities, so I was responsible for designing and implementing new programs to replace the old ones and for showing members how a fraternity could have goals relevant to modern campus life. Each chapter and campus is different, and fraternities are by nature tradition-minded institutions, so the job of innovator requires a great deal of on-the-spot problem-solving and the ability to gain confidence within a short period of time . . . .

Information that is too personal can be embarrassing, and again think of the reader! Overloaded with work, the personnel manager stuffs a résumé in his attaché case and heads for home. He kisses his wife, greets his children, pours himself a drink, loosens his tie, and reads the following:

WENDY HAZELTON
WHO IS SHE?

This is an addendum to my résumé. Admittedly, scholastic and professional background is important and tells a great deal about a person, but in presenting a character it is quite sterile. Therefore, this accompaniment: it does not tell what I am but suggests who I am.

Her greatest gift from life: A deep-seated happiness and an easy smile.

Her greatest gift to life: Openly showing the happiness so others might feel it also.

Her greatest fault: Not focusing her talents in one area. (This prevents boredom but also precludes a single expertise. She is working on corrections.)

INTERESTS

Solitude—to read and think; to develop

Music—Bach, Tchaikovsky, Rachmaninoff, Liszt . . .

Books—D.H. Lawrence, Henry Miller, Gibran, Fromm

Sewing—she makes 75 percent of her clothes, designs some

Knitting—because it is such an ancient art and fun

Cooking—only those things that take all day and taste like it (sour cream black bread!)

People—all people (especially those who are mentally alive) because of their infinite variety, their uniqueness, and amazing similarities

SHE TRIES TO:

Find one new "favorite" piece of music a month

Find one new good book a month

Find one thing that makes her glad she's alive per day

Spend a few moments whenever necessary standing back from life to give her world perspective; to understand her place in it, the place of others, and their relationship to each other—specific and holistic.

And so on. The personnel man pours himself another drink, contemplates the strange business of recruitment-by-résumé, and settles down to the serious business of searching for a qualified candidate.

What can you say about something like this? How about a summary?

Travel background

United States:	New York, New Jersey, Connecticut, Maine, Vermont, New Hampshire, Massachusetts, Delaware, Maryland, Washington, D.C., Virginia, Carolinas, Georgia, Florida, California, Texas, Nevada, Arizona, New Mexico, Louisiana, Mississippi, Alabama, Montana, Colorado, Iowa, Ohio, Indiana, Illinois, Nebraska, Wisconsin, Utah, Michigan, Pennsylvania.
North America:	Canada (Montreal resident, 1969-1970), Mexico, Bahamas.
Europe:	France (Paris resident, 1966-1967), Belgium, Portugal, Netherlands, Luxembourg, Italy, Switzerland, Great Britain; extensive travel in Spain and Greece.

A résumé is not the place to be bitter.

1962-1965	Temporary positions. At that time anyone over 30-35 was not considered hirable due to age only.

Anyone for laundry lists?

Educational background

School	Location	Dates	Major	Degree
Jericho High School	Jericho, N.Y.	1962-66	French	N.Y. State Honors Dipl.
Univ. of Wisconsin	Madison, Wis.	1969-70	French	
Univ. of Pennsylvania	Philadelphia, Pa.	1967-68 1968-69	French	B.A.

Univ. de Paris (Sorbonne)	Paris, France	1966-67 French	C.P.L.F.
Univ. de Montreal	Montreal, Canada	1969-73 French	M.A.

Employment background

Organization	Location	Dates	Supervisor
United	New York	7/70-11/71	Mr. F. Topoff
National	New York	6/68-8/69	Mr. W. McCain
E.J. Korvette, Inc.	Huntington Station, N.Y.	Summers, 1966, 1965	Mr. M. Motin
Grange Camp	Biermont, N.Y.	Summers, 1964, 1963	Mr. P. Reece

Sample résumés

Let me demonstrate how résumés can be presented in innovative ways. First, I'll show you "befores" and "afters" of two résumés and then I'll give you examples of two other strong presentations.

Otis Flagg's résumé is the first example. He may have been bright enough to have earned his M.A., but his résumé was confusing, showing fuzzy thinking and poor planning and organization. What's more, for no apparent reason, dates were missing and blocs were mispositioned and duplicated. Instead of conveying a positive impression, the résumé undermined Otis's job search. It was an impediment instead of an aid. If Otis couldn't think clearly, no prospective employer would take the time to do his thinking for him.

(BEFORE)
OTIS FLAGG

Personal Data:
Age: 25
Health: Excellent
Marital Status: Single
Mailing Address: c/o Mr. Arthur Zimmer
2019 Columbia St., Lincoln, N.D. 20008

Telephone:	(910) 842-6141 (until June 30) (262) 762-0794 (after July 1)
Present Position:	Director of Placement, Assistant to Dean of Students, and Counselor at Hobart Community College in Essex, N.Y. 28472
Position Desired:	Position with the Personnel Staff. Particularly interested in customer and employee relations; company recruitment, staffing, and placement; and employee utilization.
Special Interests:	Entering any available management training program.
Education:	M.A. in College Personnel Services with Counseling minor from the University of Florida, Gainesville, Florida B.A. in History with Psychology minor from Duquesne University, Pittsburgh, Pa.
College Honors:	Graduated Cum Laude, voted President of Junior Class and Secretary of Senior Class, twice honored in WHO'S WHO AMONG STUDENTS IN AMERICAN COLLEGES AND UNIVERSITIES.
Work Experience:	*Graduate Practicums:* Worked in the Office of Financial Aid for three months with brief additional practicums in the offices of Admissions, Placement, and Dean of Students at the University of Florida. Current Job Duties: As Director of Placement: Creating a placement office (none was present previously); acquiring and organizing career information files; devising career form letters, student card files, application forms, etc.; keeping posted on all campus programs and local job market trends; meeting with local industry representatives and securing company recruiters for campus visits; creating a special Career Night on campus for students to meet with local industry representatives (none was held previously); notifying interested students of job openings; designing a one-quarter course

on career decision-making skills and job interviewing; assisting students in career counseling, résumé writing, and interviewing techniques.

As Counselor: Working with student tutors; handling student problems related to academic course work, personal problems, and career planning; conducting 50% of all admissions interviews; helping plan student government leadership-development seminar; and generally assisting students with any problems they cared to entrust to me.

As Assistant to Dean of Students: Planning and organizing College Day and Career Night; handling problems of campus thefts; dealing with minor student problems and complaints; assisting in planning special campus events such as orientation, graduation, high school counselor workshops; and other duties as assigned by Dean of Students.

Professional Objectives: To pursue a career in personnel management.

References:
Mr. Tom T. Brown, Dean of Students
Dr. Tod Nottingham, President
Mr. Keith Hyde, Director of Special Services

Flagg, following my instructions, submitted this revised résumé:

(AFTER)
OTIS FLAGG

Address: 2019 Columbia St.
Lincoln, N.D. 20008
Telephone: (262) 762-0794

Age: 25
Health: Excellent
Marital Status: Single

Professional Objectives: Position with the Personnel Staff. Particularly interested in company recruitment, staffing, and placement; customer and employee relations; and management training programs.

Education: Master's degree in College Personnel Work with Counseling minor from the University of Florida, Gainesville, Florida, 1972.

1972 Graduate practicums included work in the Office of Student Aid for three months with additional work experience in the offices of Admissions, Placement, and Dean of Students at the University of Florida.

1970 Bachelor's degree in History with Psychology minor from Duquesne University, Pittsburgh, Pennsylvania.

Undergraduate honors included selection as President of Junior Class and Secretary of Senior Class, double mention in WHO'S WHO AMONG STUDENTS IN AMERICAN COLLEGES AND UNIVERSITIES, and graduation with 3.5 average.

Experience 1972-1973: Director of Placement, Counselor, and Assistant to Dean of Students at Hobart Community College, Essex, New York

Job Duties: As Director of Placement—Creating the college's first placement office; assisting students with career counseling, résumé writing, and interviewing techniques; notifying interested students of job openings; evaluating local job market needs; meeting with local industry representatives and securing company recruiters for campus visits; organizing a special Career Night on campus for students to meet with industry representatives; and designing an academic course on career decision-making skills and job interviewing.

As Counselor—Handling student problems related to academic course work, personal problems, and career planning; conducting 50 percent of all college admissions interviewing; working with student tutors; planning student government leadership-development seminar; and generally assisting students with any problems they cared to entrust to me.

As Assistant to Dean of Students—Dealing with minor student problems and complaints; planning special campus events such as College Day, orientation, graduation, high school counselor workshops, and student leadership seminars; handling campus thefts; and other duties as assigned by the Dean.

Now he will be heard—and listened to. This résumé will be a serious contender for positions in placement/personnel. Employers will notice his qualifications, which now stand out for readers to see instead of being hidden by poor organization.

Richard Stone also needed help in making order out of disorder. Here are his résumés.

(BEFORE)
PERSONAL DATA SHEET
APPLICANT: Richard Stone
ADDRESS: 1231 Vermont Avenue, N.W.
Apartment 604
Washington, D.C. 20605
POSITION APPLIED FOR: Writer and/or Public Relations
A. PERSONAL DATA
1. Age: 28
2. Height: 5' 9"
3. Weight: 160
4. Health: Excellent
5. Marital Status: Single
B. SIGNIFICANT WORK EXPERIENCE
1. News Reporter for *The Sarasota Ledger*, Sarasota, Florida. (3 years)
2. Business Associate with Community Action Agency of

Hillsborough County, Tampa, Florida. Work experience included management of office and employees, writing news columns, and maintaining media relations. (2 years)
3. Student reporter for *The Gainesville Sun*, Gainesville, Florida.

C. EDUCATIONAL BACKGROUND
1. Graduated with an academic degree from Boone High School, Orlando, Florida, 1963.
2. Graduated from Lake City Junior College with an Associate of Arts degree in 1965.
3. Graduated from the University of Florida in 1967 with a Bachelor of Science Degree in Journalism and Communications. Obtained a double minor in Psychology and Sociology.
4. Participated in the following college activities:
   a. Secretary of the Student Government Association.
   b. Selected for "Who's Who Among American Junior College Students."
   c. Business Manager for college yearbook.
   d. Staff writer for campus newspaper.
   e. Member of Phi Theta Kappa (academic fraternity).
   f. Member of Gamma Beta Phi Society (academic and service organization).

(AFTER)

Résumé of:	Richard Stone
Address:	1231 Vermont Ave. N.W., Apt. 604
	Washington, D.C. 20605
Telephone:	(262) 338-6299
Personal	Birth Date: July 24, 1945
Data:	Birth Place: Florida
	Marital Status: Single
Education:	B.S., 1967, The University of Florida
	Overall Grade-Point Average: 3.0 (A = 4.0)
	A.A., 1965, Lake City Junior College, Florida
	Overall Grade-Point Average: 3.2 (A = 4.0)
Extra–	Secretary of Student Government Associa-
curricular	tion, 1966-1967; Business Manager for Col-

Activities: lege Yearbook, 1965-1966; Staff Writer for Campus Newspaper, 1965-1967.

Honors: WHO'S WHO AMONG AMERICAN JUNIOR COLLEGE STUDENTS; Phi Theta Kappa Honor Fraternity; Gamma Beta Phi Honor and Service Organization; Dean's List

Additional Information: Photographic ability; Publicity Chairman for Florida's West Coast March of Dimes Fund-Raising Drive (1970-1971); Volunteer Tutor and Writer for the WASAR Community Tutoring Program, Orlando, Florida (1972).

Professional Information: News Reporter, *The Sarasota Ledger,* Sarasota, Florida: Duties included city and county government reporting, police beat reporting, feature writing, and photography. Circulation: 60,000 with three daily editions. (September, 1970-April, 1973)

Public Relations Director, The Community Action Agency of Hillsborough County, Tampa, Florida: Responsibilities included writing summary reports for government officials, writing a bi-weekly news column concerning the agency's activities, arranging press conferences, writing news releases, maintaining relations with the news media and government officials. (March, 1968-May, 1970)

Student Reporter, *The Gainesville Sun,* Gainesville, Florida: Responsible for developing story ideas, photography for publication, editing and layout of three daily editions of the paper at least twice a week. Circulation: 35,000 with three daily editions. (June, 1966-September, 1966)

When Joyce Newton wanted to change jobs, she changed cities as well. Joyce and I revised her original résumé to come up with the following result. Notice that Joyce briefly describes the organizations for which she worked for the benefit of potential employers in the new city, and that she identifies a personal reference within the text of each employment segment. When you move from one city to another, this information is helpful.

JOYCE NEWTON

Address:	Education:
c/o Sutter Hotel	Hooley Business School
562 Regent Street	Patricia Stevens Modeling School
Chicago, Illinois 64614	Skills:
Telephone:	Typing 70-80;
(312) 421-5818	Shorthand 90-100; Bookkeeping

Experience:

Hatton & Pinkney, Washington, D.C.

One of the top 200 companies in the United States, manufacturers of electric and nuclear power generators. Administrative Assistant

Duties: Handled all disbursements and purchases for Washington office. Submitted cash reports and expense reports to corporate headquarters. Assisted vice president with annual budget for the Washington office. Processed personnel records, i.e., security questionnaires, passports, and visas. Set up filing system for classified documents and correspondence. Organized library. Filled requests for various publications. Responded to inquiries for information from many government agencies. Responsible for complete office renovation. (1971-1973)

Reference: Mr. R.H. Burrows

Socio-Dynamics Industries, Inc., Washington, D.C.

A private consulting firm primarily established to work on environmental matters. It dissolved due to lack of contracts and financing.

Secretary

Duties: General office responsibilities, including correspondence, travel arrangements, and light bookkeeping. (1970)

Reference: Mr. L. Stevens

Tele-Sec Temporaries, Washington, D.C.

Worked as a temporary secretary while attempting to be-

come involved in real estate. (1968-1970)
Reference: Mrs. K. Fisher
ITT Conway, Inc., Washington, D.C.
A subsidiary of International Telephone and Telegraph Cor-
poration, manufacturing radar systems and associated elec-
tronic hardware.
Secretary to Director, Washington Operations
Duties: Performed secretarial duties and kept appointment
calendar for Director, Washington Operations. Also per-
formed secretarial duties for visiting IIT Conway executives.
Ordered office supplies and publications. Reviewed, re-
corded, and reported office expense accounts. Responsible
for travel authorizations, vacation and sick leave records.
Made airline and hotel reservations. (1966-1968)
Reference: Mr. W.D. Carter
Northern Railway System, Washington, D.C.
Assistant to Director, Personnel Development
Duties: Monitored legislation pertinent to employee rela-
tions. Gathered data on compensation and benefits. Pro-
vided information concerning educational programs offered
by universities and the American Management Association.
Reviewed and evaluated performance appraisals. Handled
recruitment and interviewed nonprofessional applicants.
Maintained personnel records. (l966)
Reference: Mr. R. Johns
World Satellite Corporation, Washington, D.C.
One of the world's largest global communications satellite system.
Personnel Assistant
Duties: Recruited, screened, tested, and interviewed applicants. Reviewed and classified all professional résumés and
forwarded them to appropriate managers. Arranged travel
and hotel accommodations for out-of-city applicants. Assisted with relocation of new employees. Conducted orientation programs for new employees. Reviewed transfers and
promotions. Handled exit interviews. Researched and drafted
personnel policies and procedures. Initiated and proposed
salary schedule. Supervised staff. (1963-1965)
Reference: Mr. B. Lewis

Somehow I always expect writers to be born communicators, never at a loss for the right word at any time. Unfortunately, Gilbert Headley, although an experienced journalist, couldn't get his résumé together. We worked on it jointly and came up with the following revision. Educational credentials were presented first to document his "license" to practice his trade. (On some occasions, however, you might want to save that goodie for the end, if it is truly a goodie—for example, if you have a degree from Yale and were editor of the daily newspaper there. Use this reverse ploy only if your *experience* is equally outstanding.)

RÉSUMÉ OF GILBERT HEADLEY

Home Address:	Office telephone:
3604 Park Drive	693-7600 Ext. 251
Alexandria, Va. 22362	Home telephone: 236-5421
Education 1960	Fordham University. Bachelor of Science Degree. Major: Journalism. Minor: American History.
	Honors and awards: Admitted to Kappa Tau Alpha, national journalism scholastic society. Awarded full-tuition scholarship by the university. Dean's List.
Employment 1968 to present	National Business Society, Washington, D.C. Writer, Editorial Staff, *National Business Magazine,* 1969 to present. Write and edit manuscripts. Evaluate staff and nonstaff material. Guide nonprofessional writers, particularly scientists, in the preparation of acceptable manuscripts.
	Writer, News Service Division, 1968 to 1969. Wrote news features for distribution to newspapers, magazines, and radio stations throughout the United States and Canada. Promoted the Society's television specials, books, museum, records, and the magazine through news releases. Wrote speeches for Society officers. Assisted news media in covering Society events.
1961 to 1968	*Washington Evening Star,* Washington, D.C.

	Reporter. Covered local, state, and national politics; city, state, and federal courts; municipal affairs.
1959 to 1961	*Herald*, Norfolk, Virginia
	Reporter. Covered U.S. District Court and various federal agencies in Norfolk area; reported on Virginia Beach area; joined staff as general assignment reporter during summer vacation from college and returned after graduation.
Achievements	Completed photography course conducted
1970	by the National Business Society for selected staff members.
1969	Honored by the Alexandria, Virginia, post of the American Legion for assisting the Crime Commission in its examination of the city's courts and police system.
Military	U.S. Navy
Service	Wrote articles and news releases and took
1952 to 1956	photographs at Public Information Offices at the Naval Air Station, Patuxent River, Maryland, and at Command Headquarters, San Juan, Puerto Rico. Edited daily and monthly newspapers aboard an aircraft carrier. Received an honorable discharge as a Journalist 2nd Class.
Personal	Born July 1, 1935, in Atlanta, Georgia. Wife: Grace K. Headley, Analyst in Social Legislation, Congressional Research Service, Library of Congress.

A résumé should always be written with as much objectivity as you can muster. Never lose sight of its function, and always keep the reader in mind. Most résumés require several revisions. First drafts should be rewritten, second drafts corrected, third and fourth drafts clarified until the final copy seems to have a life of its own. It is particularly helpful to have friends critique your résumé. Their reactions are clues that tell how well you're getting your message across.

The functional résumé

Earlier in this section I explained how to draft a résumé that promotes secondary abilities rather than primary skills. In Jon Tasha's case, you'll remember, the objective was to emphasize those qualifications in his background that would earn him consideration based on what he *knew* instead of what he *did*. And Jon did, in fact, succeed in transferring his knowledge to a new field. But what if you want to change careers completely? Perhaps you are re-entering the job market. Or, due to economic conditions, your abilities are not marketable in terms of current manpower needs? You have a special problem when you are not able to make your past part of your future. In these instances the résumé will be of little help. The more you describe what you have done, the more you lock yourself in. The more you explain what you would like to do—without evidence that you can do it—the less credible you become.

Your best gambit is to use the functional résumé. The key factor in drafting this type of résumé is to put each bloc in a sequence that shows your background in the best light possible. For example, if information in the personal data bloc is your strong suit, position it at the top. If your educational background is exceptional, give it top billing. Achievements belong first if they are outstanding, or a summary of experience may head your list if it's appropriate. And you needn't use every bloc—only those that are applicable. Whenever practical, use a *chronology of experience*: a list of previous employers, including dates of employment. It lends authenticity to your résumé. Do not indicate an occupational objective, but allow the reader to see you his way.

This is the outline for the functional résumé.

Name:
Address:
Telephone:
Summary of Experience:
Highlights of Experience:
Chronology of Experience:
Education:
Special Achievements:
Personal Data:

The following is one version of a functional résumé that skillfully presents the facts, keeping the interests of the employer in mind, without sacrificing individuality.

DOROTHY CHRISTIE
4 Ash Rd., Chester, Va.
696-5447

CHRO-NOLOGY OF EXPERIENCE:	National Association of Newscasters, Washington, D.C., 1971-73 National Center for Law, Washington, D.C., 1970 Hunt Aluminum, Washington, D.C., 1969 Farm Equipment Manufacturers Association, Washington, D.C., 1968
SUMMARY OF EXPERIENCE:	Administrative Assistant to Director of the Research and Development Division. Responsibilities: Assisted with all phases of annual convention; made hotel and travel arrangements; supervised registration; assisted with publicity and promotion. Office Manager. Duties: Recruited, screened, and interviewed applicants for positions. Briefed and trained new employees; purchased supplies and office equipment; coordinated the publication of legal manual; supervised project researchers; kept the books; wrote checks; prepared forms. Other duties: Kept records on government bids and contracts; responsible for classified documents; compiled reports; set up filing systems; billing; invoicing; supervision of mail room.
SPECIAL ABILITIES:	Social: An ability to meet and deal with people from all walks of life with ease and diplomacy. A flair for the international—having been married to a diplomat—stationed in India, Turkey, and Europe. Planning, executing, and hostessing social functions large and small.

What happens to your résumé

Your next task is to get the résumé off your desk and into the hands of an interested employer. The next four steps will bring you closer to your job: (1) prepare a cover letter; (2) select your reader with care; (3) followup; (4) choose your references wisely.

The cover letter

Why bother with a cover letter? You may wonder why you can't just fold and stuff your résumé into an envelope, seal it, stamp it, and send it off.

Very simply, if you stop to think about it for a moment, all résumés have basic similarities. Librarians' résumés are look-alikes; accountants' résumés have much in common; and so on. To get the employer to single out the "paper you," you'll have to use some ingenuity to separate yourself from the crowd.

The cover letter provides additional pertinent information and reemphasizes your qualifications consistent with the employer's needs. As your "personal messenger," it shows your uniqueness and your ability to express yourself on paper and gives a glimpse of your personality. Addressed to a real person—not "Dear Sir" or "Dear Ms.," it becomes a personal communiqué. It proves to the reader that you made the effort and used your resourcefulness to find out his name and title (the easiest way to get this information is to inquire by telephone).

The introductory paragraph of the cover letter should explain your reason for writing. Either you are responding to the company's advertisement for a particular position they want to fill, or, better yet, you are contacting him on the recommendation of Mr. So-and-so. Perhaps you are writing on your own initiative because you feel you can make a useful contribution to that organization—an excellent reason to broadcast your availability.

The next paragraph should highlight your accomplishments and achievements. The tone should be neither overly aggressive nor overly modest. Don't dilute your desirability by saying, "I have a degree in journalism, but at present I have a temporary job in a hospital." It is important to give evidence of relevant previous experience and imply the potential you offer. "My commercial art experience includes creation and design, budgeting and scheduling, and supervising a staff of four. Last year I developed a program of preplanning that saved the company $25,000." Direct and specific. It shows your awareness of profit and loss—something that's always on management's mind.

The closing paragraph must be a door-opener for further, hopefully personal, contact. Never say, "I hope to hear from you at your earliest convenience." The burden of continuing contact rests with you. You might say, "Will you see me? I'll call your office next week to determine the next step." Or, "I am available for an interview at your convenience. I'll telephone your secretary next week to make specific arrangements."

Selecting your reader

Who are the chosen people who will be the recipients of your masterful résumé and professional cover letter? Your efforts in planning and preparing your résumé will not perish if these missives are properly directed.

Although you may not believe it, you already know of quite a few people to whom you should direct your résumé and cover letter. Everybody belongs to an affinity group. Latin American specialists, electrical engineers, transportation experts, all know of a number of firms that do work similar to theirs. These are your prime targets, the organizations whose managers are qualified to assess your background, respect your capabilities, and most likely be interested in your potential.

Choose employers, colleagues, and contacts from this group and alert them to your availability. Your attitude should be that you are doing them a favor by letting them see your résumé. Don't ask for a job; offer talent. Don't look for a job opening; ask for information. Everybody, including employers, likes to be sought out for advice and assistance. If you make a person feel important, he will very likely help you promote your career.

It is a paradox that the more you think you know about companies engaged in the same work you do, the more likely you are to be reluctant to work for your "competitors" or for the opposition." Certainly I do not recommend acting contrary to your conscience or convictions, but keep an open mind.

If you have a specialty, therefore, you probably know right now who will hire you. If you don't, or if you are committed to changing fields, you have to work harder. You have no "bullseye" that is your prime target. Nevertheless, that does not give you the license to shoot your résumé off in every direction. As a matter of fact, it means you must choose your target even more carefully. Marketing your skills requires research and resourcefulness. Lois Evans wanted to get out of real estate sales because she didn't like the ups and downs of income based on commissions. She was looking for a job with stability and security. She responded to every ad labeled "Administrator" or "Public Relations" that sounded interesting. Although she was very capable in dealing with the public, she was not a PR pro, and her résumé was not competitive in the open market. Most positions for administrators required experience she lacked—supervision and familiarity with accounting or purchasing.

After a brainstorming session, we were able to develop a number of practical alternatives. One was property management and another was hotel/motel management. Both were reasonably related to the work she had done. Instead of answering ads, Lois took the initiative in contacting employers in those fields and submitting her résumé in person. Her personal appearance was an added attraction to her somewhat undistinguished résumé. One thing led to another, as it often does, and Lois was offered a position with a country club to assist the director of banquet sales. It is a very logical and appropriate job for her, and she is very good at what she does. Her finesse and tact with people are very helpful to her boss, and the steady income is welcome to her.

The more general your background, the more necessary it is to make a logical, thoughtful, rational case for your consideration. Do not send your résumé *everywhere*. Make a market research study and list specific companies you'd like to work for. Is there something unusual about your background that would be of particular interest to any of them? Can you justify sending them your résumé?

It might be helpful to review Part 2, "Your Marketability in the Job Market." Your objective at this stage is to get job *ideas*, not job *offers*. Read the *Wall Street Journal* and the business pages of your local paper; scan the Yellow Pages. Something might click. Do you know people who do what you would like to do? Talk to them. Ask questions. Get their suggestions.

Then take all the data you've gathered, all the suggestions you've gotten, all the advice you've been given, and study the information carefully. Compare one idea with the next. *Do nothing* until you decide which are the five best suggestions.

Then act. Send out a few résumés to firms that you judge most likely to be interested in your background.

Following up

Here is some advice you almost never hear, yet it is one of the most important links in your job campaign. I call it *follow-up*. It goes well beyond sending your résumé off with a cover letter indicating that you will telephone the next week to pursue matters further.

Follow-up is the constant and continual appraisal of your job search efforts. As you disseminate your résumé, you will be getting feedback. Analyze the results of your trials, errors, and dry runs. Keep records of the sources that have been most productive and the kinds of employers that have been most receptive to your résumé. List the ads you have answered and keep copies of your cover letters.

A pattern will emerge, and it will be a guide, signaling the impact your résumé is making, which of your skills are considered most marketable, and who is interested in what you have to offer. This is valuable information with which to evaluate your efforts and progress. Are you on the right track? Does your résumé need revision? Without follow-up you might spin your wheels for a long time.

Remember that the job market is an ever-changing scene and you yourself change as your search continues. The dynamics of this interaction suggest the wisdom of regularly reassessing where you are, where you've been, and how to get to where you want to be.

Choosing references

Plan your references as you plan your entire employment campaign, with loving and intelligent care. Your best friend may not be your best reference; your worst enemy may not be your worst reference. But who will be good ones?

Choose someone who knows how you function in a work situation, someone who expresses himself well and clearly, in written and verbal form. He may not endorse you 100 percent, but who believes a reference who does? He may point out that at times you are obstinate, but if he also points out that you are bright, quick to learn, and glad to confront the unexpected, he has given you a good reference that makes you sound human.

It's a fine idea to ask references for permission to use them as references—a courtesy at the very least. But by that I don't want to suggest that you should influence them. A "guided" reference is a misguided effort. Still, you can be resourceful and help your references help you. I know one enterprising aspirant for a university job who provided her transcript and a list of honors, awards, and achievements to all people contacted to write recommendations on her behalf.

A word of caution, however: don't exploit your references; save them for occasions when they will be most needed. Surprisingly, references seldom play a significant role in the hiring process. Most references are not checked until just before a job offer is made, when the prospective employer has practically made up his mind to hire the candidate. The purpose of checking references is usually for verification rather than evaluation. Reference giving and getting is a surprisingly unsophisticated procedure.

How do employers respond to inquiries about former employees? If the first question asked is "What can you tell me about Mason Aldrich?" and the reply is "Mason who?" the chances are the reference won't be a particularly good one. The employer hardly remembers the employee. But if the former employer reacts spontaneously in a voice that rings true, the result is likely to be a good recommendation.

Employers are, after all, as human as the rest of us. Their consciences make it very difficult for them to say things that would deny employment to a worker. On the other hand, they feel duty-bound to reveal information of such problems as theft or alcoholism. Prudent employers will want to know the kind of position for which the former employee is being considered. Then they are able to make more valuable assessments of the employee's capabilities.

Prospective employers react in varying ways to references. Some prefer to make the decision to hire independently, without checking references. This seems to suggest a lack of concern, interest, or trust in former employers' comments. Others make only minor effort to probe candidates' backgrounds. They ask perfunctory questions: "How long was she there?" "Did he get along with coworkers?" "Would you rehire him?" The way questions are phrased indicates a predetermined attitude toward making the candidate a job offer.

Only prospective employers who are expert in asking in-depth questions will get useful answers to help them make their decisions. My own observation is that a thorough investigation of previous employment is made most often when an employer has doubts or reservations about hiring an applicant.

So in the final analysis a good reference will help you when the employer is already predisposed to hiring you, and a poor reference may eliminate you if the employer already has reservations. Otherwise, employers, like everyone else, tend to interpret what they hear in a way that conforms with what they want to believe.

PART 5: THE ANATOMY OF HIRING

Behavioral characteristics of employers

I want to give you a behind-the-scenes glimpse of the people who hire other people.

Whenever someone gets a job, there is someone who gives a job.

Up to this point, I have discussed employment primarily in terms of *your* needs, *your* strategy, and *your* problems. Now I'm going to ask you to look at the employment picture primarily from the employer's point of view. What are *his* problems? What are *his* habits, foibles, and propensities? How does *he* view the hiring process?

"The hiring process," says one employer, "is inconsistent." "Irrational," says another. "Unpredictable," adds a personnel manager. Finding the right person to hire is, for management, just as complicated as finding the right job is for you. It stands to reason that if you have a more complete understanding of management's behavior in the hiring process, you can plan your own job-finding strategy more knowledgeably.

Let's have a look at how management copes with its hiring problems.

It begins with one of the following needs:

A. To replace an incumbent because he or she
  1. Was promoted *or*
  2. Got a better job with another firm *or*
  3. Left the area *or*
  4. Retired *or*
  5. Couldn't get along with the boss *or*
  6. Was fired.
B. To add a staff member to fill a newly created position due to
  1. Expansion *or*
  2. Favorable market conditions *or*
  3. Increased volume *or*
  4. New ventures *or*
  5. Reorganization.

If management is replacing an employee, seeking the same kind of person for the same kind of position, the hiring process is relatively simple. It is comparable to the job-seeking process of persons who are searching for positions reasonably similar to those they have had. If management changes the job description, the qualifications for the job must obviously change as well. Compare such a change with the adjustment a job seeker must make if he is looking for a position with responsibilities other than those required in his previous job.

When management creates a new position, it must first develop a blueprint, a guide to describe the position. Then it must define the type of person needed to fill the job, spelling out duties, salary, objectives, and growth potential. This applies for both entry-level and executive positions. (Of course, the more senior the position, the more complex the considerations.) Does this begin to sound familiar? Isn't this exactly what you had to do before you could launch your own job search intelligently?

There is no precise formula for management to follow any more than there is for you. The alternatives are not always crystal clear, and there are no hard and fast rules. Management is saddled with its own idiosyncrasies as you are with yours. Often it is locked into an inflexible company policy.

Management uses the same avenues for recruitment that you use for your search: classified ads, trade journals, professional affiliations, and word-of-mouth personal contacts. Interestingly, management fills more jobs through personal referrals than through any other single source.

Management is comprised of individuals, each of whom has his own set of preferences and priorities, just as you have yours. If you think making your own personal choices is difficult, multiply that by the number of individuals involved in making a corporate decision, and you can see that it becomes considerably more difficult.

Managements, like people, have their own personalities and self-images. Some are conservative and staid; others are progressive and upbeat; and all have an affinity for like-minded people (don't you?). They do what they do because they "like it that way," or they "feel it's important," or they "believe in it."

For example, some employers always advertise for positions they are trying to fill; some never do. Others advertise only for certain positions, and still others prefer blind ads. Why? "It's been successful in the past," or "We've always done it that way."

Some companies adhere slavishly to psychological testing; others to lengthy applications. Some personnel managers start reading résumés from back to front (or bottom to top), contending that that's where the least favorable information is likely to be. (And a few personnel clerks file résumés in such a way that they can never be found again!)

Many supervisors who have hiring responsibilities will probably agree that hiring poses a dilemma, particularly when there are several qualified candidates for the same position. Then what is the basis for selection—intuition?

Do employers observe their own hiring policies? Yes and no. They may say they require a master's degree for a certain position but hire a person with only a B.A. They may slot a position at one salary level and fill it at another. "No openings at this time" may be the official line, but you know that jobs have been created for unusual candidates who happen to appear even during a no-hiring period.

In short, hiring policies are followed always, often, frequently, occasionally, or never.

The time of your life

Chaotic though the hiring process may be, the job seeker does have one important tool that is a barometer to measure his or her progress. That is *time*. The efficient use of time is an indicator of how well you have organized your job-finding campaign.

For starters, remember the truism that getting a job is a matter of being in the right place at the right time. And there is always the question of the best time to look for a job. No one season is better than another, although job-hunting during holiday seasons can be particularly grim. Generally, I can't think of a better time to look for a job than when you need one. Then it matters, and time is of the essence.

Time and timing play an important role in your job search. You must get to interviews on time. (And you'll spend time waiting to be interviewed.) The very nature of an interview is affected by a time factor; leisurely interviews are far more productive than those limited by tight schedules. And the length of an interview may be a clue to the extent of the interest it has generated. Think of the time that passes while you are hoping for the phone call that brings good news of employment.

Getting hired is influenced by the element of time in more significant ways, too. For example, experience is measured in terms of time as well as proficiency. Compare the job seeker who has held two positions in seven years with the one who has held seven positions in two years. Doesn't this comparison tell you something about job stability and/or job performance?

Financial adversity can rob a job seeker of adequate time to find the best job. Expediency forces premature job choices. If you must go to work immediately, you must be prepared to accept the position available at the time. Stop-gap jobs are short-range substitutes for long-range career goals. You bide your time until times are better. Professional careers take years to build.

Most of all, the time factor is a gauge by which you can predict your prospects of a job offer once you are under consideration for a position—and by "under consideration," I mean that you have been *interviewed* for the position, not that you have simply sent out a résumé.

It may seem out of sequence to discuss being under consideration for a position before discussing interviews, but this digression is in the context of time. Studying the length of time it takes an employer to select and hire a candidate can be a subtle way of interpreting his actions during the recruitment period. It may tell you, for example, how eager he is to fill the position or even suggest how much competition you may be facing. It teaches you to be sensitive to the nuances of employers' hiring styles and to question their motivation. It will make you aware of the need to read between the lines that some employers give you.

First, the more senior the position, or the more specialized the skills required, the longer the hiring process. In your terms, this means that if you're a top-level job seeker, give yourself ample time to find a position and be found for one. After all, the job that's open today and filled tomorrow is only a garden variety job.

The résumé that is dispatched at the beginning of the week and evokes a response by the end of the week surely has found its mark. Some personnel manager read it and decided it was very interesting. The calendar is one measure—but only one—of the quality of your resume and whether it has been directed to the proper employer.

The pace that is set for finding or filling a job tells its own story. Employers might need to hire someone yesterday, but recruiting is not the only thing they do. They *do* have a business to run, so the business of filling a job might drag on. Job seekers may have a sense of urgency about finding employment and may want to spend all day at it. But after your initial efforts, you need time for your efforts to gel. Don't be overzealous. Take some time off and relax.

Time will tell whether the things an employer says he will do get done. "You're high on our list for consideration," the employer says. "We'd like to arrange a second interview so you can talk to some of the people with whom you'd be working." (Sounds encouraging.) Or he might say ". . . a second interview so you can meet some of the other members of the group." (Translation: ". . . so they can meet you.") Then there are the famous last words: "Don't call us. We'll call you."

How long do you wait before you decide that you'll call him anyway? Wait a reasonable length of time (meaning as long as you can stand it). "Been out of town," he tells you. Or, "I've been out with the flu." Or, "The fellows I want you to meet are on vacation." If he tells you that the fellows he wants you to meet are out of town on vacation and came down with the flu—forget it. They're not thinking of you seriously.

If you're told, "We're very interested in you, but frankly we're still looking," ask yourself, "If they're so interested, why are they still looking?" Generally speaking, be suspicious when decisions are delayed, but allow for the fact that the more people there are involved in the decision making, the longer it takes to make a decision. If another job offer comes along in the meantime, call and explain the circumstances honestly. Remember that when you press for a decision you will get one—yes, no, or maybe. "Maybes" are risky. If you are unemployed, act on offers in hand. A promise of a job offer in the future usually is not to be taken seriously. If the job does not materialize, neither will the paycheck.

A job is born: what it is and for whom

The evolution of the hiring process is mysterious. When people hire other people, the dynamics of human nature make uncertainty a certainty. Let's examine how one company reached a hiring decision.

Company: Pierce Mill and Rhoades Printing Co.
127 Employees

	Industrial Printing
	$8 million gross
Officers:	Hugh Pierce, President
	Martin Mill, Vice President
	Steven Rhoades, Controller
Others:	John McCoy, General Manager
	Roy Steers, Personnel Manager
	David Fletcher, Management
	Consultant

John McCoy, general manager, resigned because his doctor recommended a change in climate to alleviate respiratory complications.

McCoy would have preferred to submit his resignation to the president of the company, Hugh Pierce, because Pierce had hired him nine years ago and they talked the same language. But the company president was vacationing in the Bahamas (his winter holidays seemed to get longer and longer each year). McCoy had lunch with the controller, Steven Rhoades, and broke the news. Rhoades, in his low-key, unflappable manner, mentioned it to Martin Mill later that day.

MILL:	This is a hell of a time! Couldn't he get sick when we're not so busy?
RHOADES:	I think he'd stay through the peak season if you asked him.
MILL:	No, I don't want to. McCoy probably has too much on his mind already. We'll just move as quickly as we can to find his replacement.
RHOADES:	Don't you think we ought to wait at least till Hugh gets back?
MILL:	You gotta be kidding! McCoy's no help to us anymore. We're running a business here, not a convalescent home.
RHOADES:	Well, let's call him to clue him in. Hugh always respected John. Let's double-check to make sure he wants to hire the same type of person again.
MILL:	Steve, when are you going to accept the fact that Hugh is getting less and less interested in what

131

goes on here and depends on us more and more to keep things running? The years are creeping up on him—on all of us for that matter.

RHOADES: We might give some thought to bringing in a bright young M.B.A. with a couple of years' experience.

MILL: Yeah. He'd probably stay with us for a year or two, just long enough to use us as a steppingstone for a better job with a larger company.

RHOADES: Then the first thing we have to do is decide on the kind of man we want. Right?

MILL: Wrong. Steve, the number-one decision is how we see the *job*.

RHOADES: Well, if you want to wipe the slate clean and really start at the beginning, let's analyze our present status and what we want to accomplish.

MILL: Good point. OK. I've been meaning to discuss this with you anyway. It's been on my mind for some time. For the last three years our volume and profits have been barely inching up. You know, Steve, if I had more time to service our large accounts I think our profits would take a leap. If we recast the general manager's job, add the responsibility of customer relations, and give the next general manager responsibility for smaller accounts, I think it would be the best thing that could happen to Pierce Mill and Rhoades.

RHOADES: Now wait a minute. Do you want to turn the general manager into a supersalesman or an account executive? When will he get to manage production and operations or prepare the budget? When will he have time to supervise the staff or handle the overall planning?

MILL: Hold it. All I'm saying is customer relations. Call it customer service. It really doesn't matter what you call it.

RHOADES: Suppose, for the sake of argument, we go that route. What duties will you take away from the job?

MILL: Take away? Who's talking about taking away anything? I'm talking about adding on to it.

RHOADES: Be reasonable. Where are you going to find such a superstar? A man who can handle everything McCoy does now plus customer relations? And how much do you expect to pay?

MILL: If we find a man who can add fifty thousand dollars to our profits, isn't he worth five thousand more than McCoy is earning—say, thirty thousand?

RHOADES: Do you think Hugh would buy that? It would knock our whole salary structure out of whack.

MILL: I can handle Hugh.

RHOADES: We're getting ahead of ourselves. Let's go back to the beginning. What do we want the man to accomplish? And what areas *don't* we want him to touch?

MILL: OK. Can we agree on this? Responsible for overall operations of printing, customer relations, budget preparation, long-range planning, and of course the supervision of department heads.

RHOADES: Give me some priorities. What *must* we have and what can we live without?

MILL: Steve, listen. I figure within five years Hugh will retire. Then I'll be sitting in that office. I want a sales-minded general manager.

RHOADES: If you feel so strongly, why don't you create a new slot entirely? Why tamper with the general manager's job? It's fine as it is.

MILL: Well, I've never been completely sold on John and the responsibilities he had, nor the way he discharged them. You know we've brought some darn good people into the company. He never used them properly. Never really motivated them. That's why our turnover is so high.

RHOADES: That's exactly why we need a strong administrator, not a marketing manager.

MILL: We can go back and forth at this all day. I've got other things to do. Look, I've got an idea. Suppose we get a management consultant in here. I'll

call Dave Fletcher. He's been helpful in the past.
You brief Roy Steers. We've got to get the ball
rolling immediately.

Roy Steers, personnel manager with Pierce Mill and Rhoades
for five years, ran the personnel department with the help of two assistants. As is true of any personnel manager, recruiting and interviewing were only a small part of his duties. In fact, this is a good
time to take a look at the inner offices of a personnel department.
The department's file cabinets are stuffed with records—records of
job performance, evaluations, promotions, terminations, insurance and health, sick leave and vacations, payroll and pensions. No
small amount of time is spent keeping all these records up to date.

The manager or director spends a great deal of time on employee relations. He has orientation sessions with new employees
and arranges training programs; he makes wage and salary surveys,
negotiates with the union, handles grievances and problems involving personality clashes, conducts exit interviews, and is accustomed to coping with the typical crises that occur whenever over a
hundred people gather daily in the name of work.

The manager's contribution to the hiring process is limited. At
best he helps shape personnel policy and is responsible for the
selection of suitable candidates. To this end he evaluates candidates' backgrounds, weighing their skills, education, experience,
attitude, initiative, energy, personality, and appearance.

First, he selects candidates whose qualifications in the foregoing categories appear to meet the requirements for a particular position. Then he appraises each of those candidates in the following
terms: Will he or she be productive immediately? How much time
and effort will it require to train him for maximum job performance? Is there an agency fee? Are there relocation expenses? The
quality and quantity of his experience; his ability to interact; his
tactfulness, cooperativeness, and reliability; and the length of time
he is likely to stay with the company are also considered.

That's an overview; the personnel manager advises, admin-
isters, evaluates, and selects. He does not hire.

At Pierce Mill and Rhoades, Roy Steers was in the personnel office when Rhoades walked in and closed the door behind him. The
controller briefly gave Steers the background on finding a replace-

ment for McCoy. Steers listened, not letting on that he had gotten the news from McCoy himself the week before. (Personnel managers are usually tight-lipped about confidential information.)

Because the company was searching for a general manager, a man who would in fact be Steers's immediate boss, Steers was to play only a minor role in the hiring process. He wrote the ad:

> Medium-sized printing company seeks general manager. Salary range 25K. Shirt-sleeve operation. Resp. for production, budget, purchasing, planning. Direct and supervise staff. Ability to promote customer relations.
> Contact Roy Steers, Personnel Dept., Pierce Mill and Rhoades Printing Company, 34 River Road, Akron, Ohio, (221) 227-4700.

It was placed in the local newspapers, the *Wall Street Journal*, and the printing trade's publication, *The Printing World*. Then Steers searched through the résumé file, but he came up with only one possibility. "Better wait and see what the ads generate," he thought. And he put aside the yellowed résumé to be compared later on with those of other candidates.

In the meantime Marty Mill had a lengthy discussion with Dave Fletcher, the management consultant. Fletcher had made an efficiency study of Pierce Mill and Rhoades the year before and had successfully recruited candidates for them as well. He knew the company's limitations as well as its potential and understood management's policies. He took the job information, inquired about the type of person most likely to fit in, asked whether the salary was flexible, and tried to pin Mill down as to which requirements were negotiable and which were non-negotiable. Previous printing experience was a must, but salary was negotiable. Fletcher promised to have some candidates lined up within a short time.

The executives sought suggestions from the printing industry association, from printing equipment manufacturers, and even from competitors. Rhoades mentioned the hunt to a paper products salesman and Mill told a client.

So the search was launched. Finding the right man, especially for an important position, is serious business. A company is only as successful as the people it employs.

In all, the company received 109 résumés. Of the 97 responses to the newspaper ad, all but four were eliminated—primarily because the candidates had had no previous printing industry experience. (The ad had neglected to spell out that requirement specifically, but applicants should have realized that they would face strong competition from others with that experience.)

Two eminently qualified candidates were developed. Fletcher brought in a general manager of a larger printing company in Dayton. The paper products salesman suggested the other candidate—the number-two man in a large national trade association who administered its printing operation in addition to other managerial responsibilities.

Both men were interviewed and re-interviewed, wined and dined. Both had excellent references and were interested in the position at the stated salary. Both were told that they were finalists and that a decision would be made soon.

"How can we hire the trade association man? He's not profit-motivated," Mill asked Rhoades.

"But I'm not entirely convinced that the fellow from Dayton is our man. I don't want anyone telling us how to run our business!" Rhoades confessed.

"How right you are," said Mill, "but in any case why don't we wait until Pierce gets back next week and see what he might have on his mind, if anything."

"If I can't get more heat in my office, I'm going back to the Bahamas," Hugh Pierce told Mill and Rhoades on his first day back.

"Hugh, you look as if you've had enough sun to hold you till the snow melts," Mill said.

"I'll bet you were on the golf course every day."

"You're right, Steve. As a matter of fact, I teamed up with a mighty fine player," Pierce continued. "Do you remember Harris Burnfield? With Flair Printing. Remember in 1971 he took a big account away from us. He's as sharp a manager as he is a golfer. I'd really like him on our team if we ever need anybody of that caliber—I think he'd come, too."

And he did.

What can I say after I've said that the hiring process is an unpredictable phenomenon? This example was, to be sure, an unusual case, but things do happen that way. Part of the confusion resulted from the fact that the key executives never fully crystallized their thinking about the job to be filled. But this is a common failing. Job descriptions are only words until they're applied to real-life situations. I've been told over and over by employers, "We ourselves didn't have a full understanding of the job until we interviewed several candidates."

Furthermore, the fuzzy job description in the classified ad was a goof. If some employers make the hiring process more difficult than it need be, they must hold themselves responsible.

Amazingly enough, despite all the vagaries of hiring, the employer quite frequently hires the right person for a given job. (At least in his opinion he has selected the most suitable candidate. In the process, other qualified or even more qualified candidates may have been passed over.)

Frequently, a guideline for hiring is that suitability for a position takes precedence over the ability to perform the functions of that position. Those very intangible ingredients called *compatibility* and *ability to fit in* weigh heavily in the final hiring decision. If one hundred people apply for a job, therefore, the ninety-nine who were not selected must keep this thought in mind: personal professional competence may not be in question; external factors may determine the criteria for selection.

What does all this mean to the job seeker? What can you do about it? All you can do is improve your job-offer possibilities by:

1. Finding out as much as you can about the employer. Is there mutual ideological agreement?
2. Learning as much as possible about the job. Is it one with which you can identify?
3. Looking at the hiring process from the employer's point of view. Are your self-image and the company image in harmony?

On the telephone: prologue to an interview

For job-hunting purposes the telephone is an instrument to use for *arranging* interviews, not *conducting* them. Many job seekers believe that if they call an employer about a job opening or a possible job opening they can save a lot of time. Yes, they may gain time, but they may lose an interview. It's risky to introduce yourself to an employer by telephone. Too many job seekers blow it.

If you want only information, write to the company and ask for its literature. If you want to know whether an employer might be interested in a person with your qualifications, send your résumé with a cover letter to the proper person. Then at least in a follow-up telephone call that person can speak more knowledgeably.

When you call an employer to apply for a position choose your words carefully, and give only enough information to create interest. Save the details for the interview. After all, you don't know the person with whom you are speaking. It is easy to lose your listener by telling too much too soon. Don't get involved in an exchange of questions and answers. You may get the wrong answers or, even worse, ask the wrong questions.

More significant than your call to an employer is his call to you. Suppose he has received your résumé, is impressed by it, and wants some questions answered before arranging an interview. This is the overture to your live interview presentation. Your telephone performance sets the stage for other, personal dialogues.

Once the employer actually appears, even as a disembodied voice, mark his words well. Really listen. What is he telling you? Ask yourself why he is asking each question. For example, if he wants to know whether you are available for employment immediately, he is not really inquiring about your timetable—*his* is in question. Or if he asks, "How much traveling are you accustomed to doing?" he is saying that the job requires a great deal of traveling. Otherwise, the subject would not come up. If he asks a question concerning salary, handle it as delicately as possible. Speak in generalities, or use a range. Say, "Salary is not my number-one concern" or, "I was hoping to get as close to fifteen thousand as I could."

It is not likely that the employer will ask any in-depth questions. He is merely checking certain points to be sure he should consider your candidacy seriously enough to interview you personally. For your part, this is not the time to ask for detailed information about the company or the position. You should have some of it already, and the subsequent interview itself will provide the rest.

Don't get into a hassle like this:

EMPLOYER: Is three o'clock Thursday a convenient time for
                 you to come for an interview?
JOB SEEKER: Thursday. Is that the eighteenth?
EMPLOYER: No, it's the nineteenth.
JOB SEEKER: Oh, of course! Could you possibly see me later in
                 the day? Or earlier?
EMPLOYER: How about ten o'clock? Or four-thirty in the
                 afternoon?
JOB SEEKER: If I can make it at ten, I'll call first. Otherwise, if
                 you don't hear from me, I'll be there in the
                 afternoon.
EMPLOYER: That sounds a little vague. Will you please call in
                 any case?
JOB SEEKER: I'll tell you what—I'll come at three on Thursday
                 the nineteenth.
EMPLOYER: Fine. (To himself: Why didn't you say so in the first
                 place!)

If you want the employer to think well of you, you must think of the employer. At this stage let him lead, and you follow. Wait for the interview to take initiatives.

The interview

Two people face each other across a desk. One asks himself, "Is this the person I want to work for?" And the other asks himself, "Is this the person I want to work for me?" An interview has just begun.

Within five minutes the employer tells himself, "This might be my man." The applicant thinks, "This might be my job." Employer and applicant are getting through to each other; they're on the same wavelength. Each one senses his responsibility to discuss in a mature, intelligent, and realistic way his own interest to employ or be employed by the other.

The good interview is a dialogue, not a monologue. The candidate must prove to the employer that he can make a useful contribution to him. He must present evidence of his successes and achievements in his previous employment in particular and in other related activities as well. He should convey that he has made an effort to familiarize himself with the company, that he understands the nature of the position for which he is being interviewed, and that he is actively interested in it.

On the other hand, if a company hopes to attract men and women who offer superior skills and attributes, it must be ready to show its concern for a candidate's needs. The employer should provide pertinent information about company policy, aims, and history. He should explain clearly the lines and limits of responsibility and the overall organizational structure. The employer should point out the positive features of the position without overlooking its negative aspects. Both must consider the future they may be sharing. Each is investing in the other.

All this must be expressed in a conversation that flows easily and naturally. It takes the talent of a diplomat, a public relations executive, a psychologist, a magician. It takes everything you've got.

Just how honest will employer and applicant be with each other? If they are going to be working with each other, surely they must be candid to a certain extent. Each one must feel that he can speak freely. But candor must be mixed with caution, for too much openness is likely to threaten anybody's credibility. The applicant cannot expect to hear confidences in regard to internal politics and personalities. These private matters are reserved for members of the firm. Every organization has problems it does not flaunt.

Conversely, every applicant is allowed to present himself as favorably as possible without being expected to dwell on his negative characteristics. He must remember, though, that he will be answerable for his boasts and must have reasonable explanations for his limitations. The interview itself is the vehicle for evaluating the performance of the aspirant. That's why it is all-important.

As employer and applicant sense a feeling of rapport, they begin to relax. Subtly, each begins to express his individuality during their give and take, and each begins to get a picture of the other as a *person*. Questions begin to probe more deeply into the intangible aspects of work—standards, styles, and values.

As you know, skills alone won't get you the job. A job means involvement. People who get involved with each other have things in common, though their strengths and weaknesses may be complementary. (In terms of job roles, inflexible bosses may prefer flexible assistants, and highly creative employees may need more disciplined bosses.)

Before a job can be offered or accepted, employer and applicant must make an earnest effort to get beneath surface assumptions. Underlying attitudes must be explored—approaches to problem-solving, abilities to get along with coworkers, thresholds of pressures and crises.

Each party must produce thoughtful and meaningful questions and answers, not canned answers to canned questions. "What do you know about the company?" is not a question to be taken lightly. Job aspirants must demonstrate that they are enlightened. "Why do you want to make a change?" must be answered legitimately and logically, if not completely accurately. There is no need for the applicant to reveal secrets that may reflect badly on himself. He doesn't have to confess that he didn't get along with the head of the department. He should leave unsaid as much as possible and instead address himself to future objectives. No interview is complete unless both parties look to the future realistically, one making a commitment to job performance, the other a commitment to job potential.

Each question and each answer adds another insight into the suitability of the person for the position and the position for the person. The applicant is being judged on his ability to marshal his thoughts and organize his ideas. How he expresses himself is equally important. Is he intelligent? Vague or concise? Pompous or informal? Aggressive or modest? Assertive or shy? In an interview the demeanor of the individual is being closely observed.

Both the applicant and the employer are revealing something of their inner selves in this game of matching wits. What kind of personality does the employer have? Is he intelligent, vague, aggressive? Does he have charm, fair-mindedness, a sense of humor?

Even under the best conditions the atmosphere of an interview is charged with stress. Important decisions hinge on its outcome. Applicants are hired for many reasons, and it may surprise you to learn that the most important is compatibility. Employers can easily catalogue candidates' qualifications. Applicants can easily enumerate job benefits. But in the end it comes down to both saying, "I like him." The chemistry is right.

What follows now are reasonable facsimiles of three interviews. You've already met the candidates: Sheila Myer, assistant
editor; Mary Capra, office manager; and Charles Wright, financial
analyst.

Let me brief you quickly before the first interview begins.
Sheila Myer responded to an ad in a trade journal for an assistant
editor's position on the staff of *World Review*. She is interviewed by
Robert Ingram, administrative assistant to the publisher.

Ingram is one of those hard-to-get-along-with types.

INGRAM:	Come in, Miss Myer. Glad to see you. I'm search-ing for your résumé. I know it's here on my desk somewhere. I understand you're an editor.
MYER:	Yes. I've been an assistant editor of University Press. We publish texts in the field of foreign affairs.
INGRAM:	I'm quite familiar with University Press; you don't have to tell me anything about that. Tell me about your background.
MYER:	I have edited solicited manuscripts and have been the first reader of unsolicited manuscripts for five years. I make recommendations for revision of texts. I correspond with writers and our printers and coordinate schedules. You might say I pro-cess manuscripts through all the stages—from author to reader.
INGRAM:	Yes. But what makes you think you're qualified for our position?
MYER:	Perhaps you can give me additional details about the position . . . .
INGRAM:	Did you read the ad?
MYER:	Yes. The ad indicated that the requirements for the position included previous experience in editing, which I have; familiarity with inter-national issues, which I have; and the ability to work with layout and makeup, which I've done.
INGRAM:	What other experience do you have?
MYER:	I was editor of my college literary magazine, and

	when I graduated from Wellesley I went to work immediately for Beacon Publications.
INGRAM:	Well, I don't think much of Beacon.
MYER (controlling herself):	Naturally your ad didn't cover all there is to tell about the position. If you will spell out some of the details—
INGRAM:	I'm sorry to hear that you feel that way about the ad because it so happens I wrote the ad myself. I thought I made myself perfectly clear.
MYER:	I should have guessed it!
INGRAM:	It is a policy here that anybody we may ask to join our staff is seen by me first. Now I will pass along your papers with my comments to our editor.
MYER:	I don't think that will be necessary, Mr. Ingram. You see, I don't believe that I would be happy working for *World Review.*

An interview like this that lacks rapport hardly deserves to be called an interview. You may wonder why Sheila didn't want her papers to be passed on to the editor, who might have been a charming, gifted man, who might even have discovered that Sheila was the ideal candidate. In this case we must respect Sheila's judgment. She was there. In other circumstances, waiting to meet the person for whom you would actually work might be a better decision.

In the next example Mary Capra lets opportunity slip through her fingers when she responds to the request "Tell me more about yourself." As you may recall, Mary was dissatisfied with her job as office manager of a law firm and was attempting to parlay her peripheral skills in physical education and recreation into a career in the health field.

Mary had read in the newspaper about a suburban Health Maintenance Organization, a newly established preventative facility with a staff of fifty-five, and submitted an unsolicited résumé. Paul Steinberger, its controller and personnel manager, was so impressed with her background that he invited her in for an interview, hoping she might be just the one to be his assistant. He needed someone to supervise four people and prepare monthly financial statements, control cash flow, prepare taxes, purchase supplies, and handle payroll, insurance records, and client relations. Here's the interview:

CAPRA:	Mr. Steinberger, I'm Mary Capra.
STEINBERGER:	Very glad to meet you, Miss Capra. Please sit down. Did you have any trouble finding us?
CAPRA:	None at all. I'm so anxious to hear all about the job. When you called I just dropped everything and flew.
STEINBERGER:	Did you have an opportunity to look around when you came in?
CAPRA:	No, I really didn't. You know I read that article in the newspaper and that gave me a picture of what you do here. I've always wanted to get into the health field.
STEINBERGER:	I can't think of a better way of getting into the health field than by being with an organization concerned with health maintenance. What do you know about HMO?
CAPRA:	I know that it has a unique approach to maintaining good health—a preventative approach. And your services differ from traditional clinic facilities.
STEINBERGER:	You've expressed it very well. We have a staff here of almost sixty, half professional, half support. We're growing and expect to add more personnel. As personnel officer, I feel it's important that I have an associate who can help us grow effectively. Your experience seems to fit my needs exactly.
CAPRA:	That's wonderful. Can you tell me something about the health services that you provide? For example, in the article I read about the library you maintain. That sounds like a marvelous way to keep your members up to date on current information.
STEINBERGER:	First let me tell you about our job. As you can imagine, it's much the same as the position you now hold—

CAPRA: I've been trying to make a transition into this field, health. Health has always been important to me. I was a physical education major. True, that goes back some. But even now I'm active, doing what I can in my free time—working with youth groups at recreational centers, giving swimming instructions to handicapped children, and planning activities for senior citizens. Now I want my job to be more meaningful, too.

STEINBERGER: I understand. In our work, using the skills and abilities that you have combined with your interest in our field, I'm sure you'll find a great deal of satisfaction here. We particularly need support in cash flow and taxes, and you're strong in those areas. Insurance forms won't be a problem, will they?

CAPRA: I've handled all sorts—in every size, shape, and color.

STEINBERGER: Of course we'd be working together as a team. I'd like to know more about your background. Your résumé says a great deal in a few words; that impressed me. But suppose you tell me more about yourself.

CAPRA: I'm dying to get into the health field. That doesn't sound right. Let's say I'm a health freak. Really, I am. As a matter of fact I've been studying to be a physical therapist. My goal is to move out of office management and administration and into supportive health services. I hope I can do just that here. It's exactly what I want.

STEINBERGER: I think you've touched on something very pertinent here, Miss Capra. It—I'm very much in need of an assistant—and an assistant in the business affairs of this health organization is going to be just exactly that. It would hardly seem likely or logical for me to be extremely interested in you, and I am, and to hire you knowing that your objectives and my needs are poles apart.

CAPRA: You gave me the impression, though, that as you grow you'll need more help in supportive ser-

vices, and I thought I could move into your physical therapy unit.

STEINBERGER: But this is the job I need you for, and it's a full-
time responsibility. I admire your desire, but I
must go back to my needs. I'm in need of what
you do—not what you want to do.

Cut! The interview is collapsing. What went wrong? "Tell me
more about yourself" means to give the employer more convincing reasons to hire you. If only Mary hadn't forecast her future plans
with so much certainty!

The very reason that an interview is such a delicate process is
that both parties are making a commitment to the future. Judg-
ments are based on projections of current information, and the hiring decision is actually made in the face of many unknowable
factors. Mary spelled out her future objectives prematurely. Who is
to say in fact what might come to pass? Mary might replace her boss
in certain circumstances—if he gets promoted, for example. Or she
might lose interest in the physical therapy program. In any case the
possibility for transition exists at HMO, and Mary couldn't help but
learn more about the health field. She would have been wiser to see
the position initially from the employer's point of view, hoping that
time and initiative might open the door to fulfilling her own goals.

Here is what might have happened had Mary described her
background in terms of the job's requirements.

STEINBERGER: . . . tell me more about yourself.

CAPRA: As you can see I've had only two jobs in fifteen
years. In both instances my responsibilities increased, from simple accounting to financial
statements, from personnel record-keeping to
interviewing and hiring. A job with growth potential means a great deal to me.

STEINBERGER: The position here is directly related to what you
have done in the past. As we grow there will be
certain changes. The time will come when this department's routine is stabilized. Then you might
want to explore assisting in other areas—the library, for example.

CAPRA:	I really appreciate your open-mindedness.
STEINBERGER:	You're the kind of person I'd like to have working for me. What are your salary requirements?
CAPRA:	Is there a range that *you* have in mind, Mr. Steinberger?
STEINBERGER:	Because you have maximum experience for this job, I'm prepared to offer you the top of the range. Fifteen thousand.
CAPRA:	That's very satisfactory. I'm earning thirteen thousand now.
STEINBERGER:	When can you start?
CAPRA:	I'd like to give three weeks' notice if it won't put you in a bind.
STEINBERGER:	The first of next month, then? Here's some background material about our organization. You may not have seen it yet. I'd like you to look through it in the meantime. It may help you a little.
CAPRA:	Thank you. I'm sure it will. I am looking forward to working with you.

The course of an interview is fluid. It changes as actions and reactions influence each other. If you can control an interview, you can better make happen what you want to happen.

Remember Charles Wright? He graduated from Rutgers and began his career as an accountant at Pace Witthouse. After four years he took an M.B.A. at Wharton School of Business and went with Jersey Stanco as a financial analyst. Now he has been wooed and won by Inter-Continental Oil. ICO needs an assistant director of international finance. The responsibilities are economic analysis, investment strategies, financial planning, administration, and liaison between the legislative department and operations research.

Dick Schumacher, ICO's treasurer, originally "discovered" Charles. During a first interview they spent hours together exploring mutual possibilities. The outcome was fruitful, and a second meeting was arranged—lunch with Wayne Oliver, vice president for international affairs; and George Leland, director of international finance and Charles's potential boss.

During the course of these talks, the men had agreed that

Charles met all the requirements for the job and that they were all interested in his assuming the position. This is a recap of his third and final interview—one with his boss-to-be, George Leland. This go-around is merely the last look at Charles Wright, the man. After all, Leland needs the right man, just as much as Wright wants the right job. In fact, Leland has already decided that he will offer the job to Wright, and Wright has already decided that he will accept. This meeting is held so that each man can confirm his decision. Now they discuss substantive issues, long-range objectives, and work styles.

WRIGHT: Here's that report you let me read. It's staggering. First the government underestimated the demand for oil and then compounded its lack of foresight by overestimating oil production.

LELAND: Even if the forecasts had been accurate, the damned trouble is that these reports are out of date before the ink is dry.

WRIGHT: The bureaucrats couldn't have foreseen all the monetary implications of an energy crisis but they sure could have foreseen the crisis itself. Inter-Continental knew it. Stanco knew it.

LELAND: Nobody listened. Well, it's time those Washington bureaucrats came up with a long-term federal energy policy. And they'd better keep the financial facts of life in mind. By the way, I expect to be giving testimony before Congress soon, and I'll need help regarding the financial implications of this problem.

WRIGHT: You know I've met some FEO people already. They're just beginning to flex their muscles.

LELAND: We're going to have to tackle the problems of depletion allowances and tax shelters. Oliver got a very favorable impression of you the other day at lunch. And I've certainly checked your background thoroughly.

WRIGHT: Then you've found me out!

LELAND: I have, Chuck. You and I both know about glow-

	ing references. But seriously, I can use a strong administrator like you.
WRIGHT:	I learned long ago that one of the best ways to run a department is to have a good communications system. That means getting ideas from the staff as well as giving instructions to them.
LELAND:	The job is going to involve more than our own department. You see, there's a sticky situation here. Our legislative research division knows its stuff all right when it comes to policy and politics, but they're not specialists in finance.
WRIGHT:	So either the financial analysts have to listen to the lobbyists or—preferably—the other way around.
LELAND:	Exactly. That's why I need someone I can depend on. I want more contact with that division, and I want you to be my representative.
WRIGHT:	Meaning that you want to put some pressure on the lobbyists.
LELAND:	Let's just say this—we need some changes here. Do you have a strong constitution? It could be a rough fight.
WRIGHT:	Strong enough. And I believe in sticking with the leader.
LELAND:	That's what they told me about you. That's why I'm putting it on the line.
WRIGHT:	Thanks for your confidence. Believe me, it's not misplaced.
LELAND:	I have a couple of practical questions. First, when can you join us? Assuming that you have decided to come aboard.
WRIGHT:	I have. I'm winding down a project that I think I can get out from under within a month.
LELAND:	Fine. The other question—has Dick Schumacher discussed salary with you?
WRIGHT:	Yes. We agreed on thirty-seven thousand.
LELAND:	Well, I'd like to add—if all goes well, and I think it will—you can expect that figure to be going up the first of the year.
WRIGHT:	That's good enough for me. I have a question.

	Would it be OK for me to sit in on your next staff meeting just so that I can get my feet wet?
LELAND:	Sure. I'll give you a call early in the week. Chuck, it looks as though everything's going to work out just fine.
WRIGHT:	Thanks. I feel it's right, too.

You don't have to be a candidate for assistant director of international finance to recognize that an interview is going well when personal issues are discussed. Nor do you have to be an executive to realize that you and a would-be employer are on the same wavelength. When these things occur, when both parties are looking at the job the same way and see the same things, then you know it's for real.

More about interviewing techniques

Interviewing skills are not easily mastered, and the art of self-presentation requires practice. This section is a review and a restatement of the principles.

First, here is a brief interview in which Mr. Stevens, the applicant, breaks at least ten basic rules governing interviewing techniques. Can you find the errors?

FORREST:	Mr. Stevens, please sit down, I'm Dennis Forrest, personnel administrator. I received your letter inquiring whether we have any job openings, and your Form 171. Did you fill in our company application?
STEVENS:	Well, I was a little late, and I didn't want to detain you any longer. Sorry, but I didn't complete it.
FORREST:	We do have certain set procedures we follow. Suppose I told you that we require all prospective employees to sit for a battery of tests. What would you say?
STEVENS:	Oh, I'd say you were putting me on.
FORREST:	It's company policy. Are you familiar with our company?

STEVENS: Well, you know—I know as much as the next fellow. You manufacture parts, right? Electronics parts.

FORREST: Mr. Stevens, we manufacture entire systems and radar sets.

STEVENS: What about the company benefits?

FORREST: I think we should both assume there are more pertinent things to discuss first.

STEVENS: I suppose you would like to know why I'm leaving my last position. Maybe you read about it in the papers. I was RIFed—reduction in force. I still can't believe it.

FORREST: Suppose you tell me about the nature of your work at NSSA.

STEVENS: Well, I've been responsible for supervising sixteen employees. I feel I know everything there is to know about contract administration. I planned and directed the operations of the department.

FORREST: Yes, fine, but can you be specific about your duties?

STEVENS: Well, it's all in the Form 171 I sent you. I was empowered with the authority to determine qualitative and quantitative requirements—

FORREST: Yes, Mr. Stevens, but what did you do?

STEVENS: Oh, you mean contracts administration. Yes, oh, using weighted guideline methods, analyzed contractors' proposals and quotations, interpreted prime contracts, and monitored performance.

FORREST: Mr. Stevens, can you outline briefly the details of your background leading up to your present position?

STEVENS: Sure, sure. You can see from my 171 that I graduated from American University in 1958 and in September of that year I went to work for the Allied Manufacturing Company. Actually, I didn't report to work until October due to a recurrent knee injury I suffered in my senior year—too much right guard. I don't mean the underarm spray! Varsity team. Well, anyhow, this old knee

	hasn't put me out of action yet.
FORREST:	Did you lose much time from your job because of it?
STEVENS:	I never really used up all my sick leave, if that's what you mean. I should have an operation, but I suppose I'll have to put it off for a while—that and a lot of other things.
FORREST:	You were about to tell me about your position with the Allied Manufacturing Company.
STEVENS:	Do you know anything about that company? There was a man there named Barrett—head of purchasing. No, his name was Bartlett. Well, anyway, he could win a prize in a tough boss contest. We never got along, and when the chance came to go with NSSA I jumped at the opportunity.
FORREST:	What were your duties at Allied Manufacturing Company?
STEVENS:	I approved supply and purchase requisitions, reviewed status reports on shipments, and analyzed charges incurred.
FORREST:	What types of equipment did you purchase?
STEVENS:	It was mostly raw materials, ferrous and nonferrous.
FORREST:	We're looking for a contract administrator for our Lanham location, but that operation will be transferred to the Atlanta facility sometime within the next twelve to eighteen months. Are you free to relocate?
STEVENS:	Oh, I couldn't do that! I own my own home and my sons are just entering high school.
FORREST:	Mr. Stevens, have you had any offers from other companies?
STEVENS:	Well, practically. As a matter of fact, General Allied promised to give me an OK tomorrow.
FORREST:	I think you ought to take it.
STEVENS:	Why do you say that?
FORREST:	Because it seems they can do more for you than we can, but thank you for coming in and good luck.

It's easy to criticize when you weren't the person who was on the spot. You probably noticed that Stevens made these mistakes:

1. He sent a government Form 171 to a private company. (Bad form.)
2. He was late. (Also bad form.)
3. He didn't complete the company application. (Uncooperative.)
4. He didn't do his homework and learn about the company. (Unprepared.)
5. He was vague about his previous experience. (Employers appreciate obtaining the facts and having them presented concisely.)
6. He said, "It's all in the Form 171." (This suggests that the interviewer did not do *his* homework; also employers want to see how you think on your feet.)
7. He gratuitously offered unrelated information concerning health. (Put your best foot forward—the healthy one, of course.)
8. He criticized his former boss. (This reflects more critically on *him*.)
9. He was unwilling even to consider the possibility of relocation. (This suggests inflexibility.)
10. Stevens appeared totally insensitive to the man who interviewed him. (He should have been thinking, "Where is this conversation going? And what is this man trying to tell me?")

You've surely been warned not to be late for your interview, but has anyone ever advised you not to be early, either? Why advertise your anxiety or your lack of other things to do?

You have also heard that the first five minutes of an interview create the atmosphere in which the interview will be conducted. The participants set the tone and form first impressions. Although first impressions are no more and no less than that, they can be hard to alter, and changing them requires concentrated effort and finesse and takes time from subjects that might otherwise be discussed.

Remember that the interviewer has the initial advantage. He or she has at least a general idea of the type of person needed. Listen closely to the interviewer, because you are in effect simultaneously interviewing him. You cannot make your own impact until you have an understanding of his needs and objectives.

Also, it's always helpful to be sensitive and responsive to the interviewer's personality. In the game of matching wits psychology plays an important role. No one can prescribe behavior—yours or the interviewer's. How to communicate best depends on your mature judgment of each interviewing situation. Different employers express themselves differently, and what they consider important differs as well.

Anticipate questions. Be a step ahead; think of what you will say to certain questions before they are asked. Those catchy questions, "What do you know about our company?" "Why do you want to make a change?" "Where do you see yourself in five years?" must be answered in terms of the employer's interests. His real interest in you emerges after he has discovered that you have what he wants.

Show interest, and go after each opportunity as if you really want the job. If you do, say so; if not, be amicable. Don't burn your bridges behind you. During your career your path and the employer's may cross again.

Be honest about your limitations. Don't try to talk yourself into a job you don't think you can do, unless, of course, you're convinced that you can learn what needs to be learned in a relatively short time. On the other hand, turn your liabilities into assets. For example, if you think you might be suspect for job-hopping, point out how each change represented increased responsibility, if it happens to be true. Take every opportunity to present your achievements, your successes. Call on your abilities as well as your experience to sell yourself. Be positive; accentuate the things you have in common with the employer.

Now is the time for you to express your goals and objectives—realistically. Discuss the job's potential and your own opportunities for the future. If you're on an executive level, inquire about the anticipated growth and long-range plans of the company.

Then comes the moment you have been waiting for, a discussion of the salary range and the benefits. The figure is discussed in the interview, negotiated when the job offer is made, and finalized when you accept the position.

"Do you have any questions?" That's your cue that the interview is coming to a close. If you can't think of an intelligent question to ask at that point (because everything has been covered), at least make an intelligent statement. Do not raise any questions concerning restrictions or conditions for employment you may have until you are offered the position.

After that, there's nothing left to do except say, "Thank you" and "Goodbye."

Before the job offer is made

The door closes, the interview is over. Now what? Need a cigarette, a cup of coffee, a drink? Relax and get comfortable. While it's still fresh in your mind, reconstruct the events of the interview. This is what I call the "waiting game."

Make a list and check the plusses and the minuses of what occurred:

1. What was your impression of the employer?
2. How do you evaluate objectively the company's interest in you? (Force yourself to accept the possibility that you might have competition for the job.)
3. How long was the interview?
4. Were you introduced to other staff members?
5. Were you shown where you would work?
6. What was *not* discussed in the interview?
7. What further arrangements were made?

There is no set pattern to an interview; therefore, there is no right or wrong answer to any of these questions. They are merely guides to help you review how it all happened.

You can do other things as well. For example, you might write a letter to the employer (if you think it's appropriate) expressing your continuing interest and giving him some *new* reasons for hiring you. Check with those whose names you have given as references. If they have been called, then the hiring process is proceeding. (The converse is not necessarily true, however. If they have *not* been called, it does not always mean that the hiring process is at a standstill.)

Don't try to psych out what's happening. It's unproductive. Be guided by what the employer does, not by what he says. Does he act or does he give excuses?

Do some further checking into the company, the person you'd be working for, and the position you hope to be offered. Compare the data with facts about other jobs you may expect to be offered. List the positives and the negatives of the job. Are the working conditions suitable to your needs? Does the job meet your most important expectations? Which of your needs are negotiable? Which are not?

Decide whether you will accept the position if it is offered.

The job offer

The job offer is like a poker game—played close to the vest. Employer and employee-to-be are trying to read who has the winning combination.

The rule of thumb for this jockeying is that the person who is more anxious that the offer be acceptable is the conciliatory one. For example, if you really want the job, you may be flexible on salary. If the employer really wants you for the position, he may stretch the salary he offers to meet your desired figure.

When the job offer is made and the salary is indicated, try to consider your desired salary, the minimum salary for which you would work, and your present salary, and come up with an average acceptable salary. If you question whether the figure offered is equitable, try to peg what your immediate superior and the person just below you in the organizational hierarchy are earning. Consider the rate and frequency of salary increases, and remember that a starting salary is only that.

Add up the benefits—vacation and sick leave; hospitalization and other insurance policies; pension; bonuses; profit-sharing; stock options, education allowances; travel expenses; credit cards; club membership; car.

As this is written, fringe benefits paid by some employers average over eleven dollars per day per employee! Take out your calculator; that's a tidy sum.

If you feel you deserve and/or need more money, explain and justify your reasons.

1. You have earned more money previously in a similar job.

2. You have superior qualifications for the job and therefore the company will benefit from your contribution.

3. You will forego a six-month salary review (assuming it's offered) if the starting salary is increased.

4. You've just been offered a higher salary with another company.

If you have another job offer that you are considering simultaneously and that pays more money but interests you less, I recommend that you accept the position that will offer greater satisfaction. In the long run it's even better than money.

If you are offered a position that is not your first choice, diplomatically delay your decision. Then, provided it is prudent, notify the other employer and apprise him of the situation. Sometimes it will hasten a favorable answer, sometimes not. Be very careful—don't jeopardize the offer you already have.

When all is said and done, and when that question—when can you start?—is finally popped, I believe if you have gone about your job search in a rational and logical way, you can then let yourself be guided by your feelings. Can you see yourself working for that company doing that job? Do you like the person you'd be working for? If the answers to both are yes, take it.

After the job offer: acceptance

The search has ended, and there's a new job waiting for you—a new beginning. Be optimistic when you accept your job. But be realistic and compromise if you must. Then give your best effort to your job and enjoy the rewards.

A job is more than a way to earn your daily bread. The intangible benefits go well beyond mere compensation. A job provides a way to earn respect and recognition. A job stimulates your creativity and resourcefulness. It is a vehicle for developing a strong sense of self. A job offers security and the promise of success for now and the future.

Of all the words written on the subject of securing employment, the most important are: *I found the right job!*

Good luck!

INDEX

160